Earn
HUGE
RETURNS *from*
PROPERTY INVESTMENTS

Earn HUGE RETURNS *from* PROPERTY INVESTMENTS

Tips to earn maximum rent. Buying real estate properties with little cash. Tips on choosing the best residential properties. Real estate investment opportunities that will make you rich.

ALEX LEE

EARN HUGE RETURNS FROM PROPERTY INVESTMENTS

Tips to earn maximum rent. Buying real estate properties with little cash. Tips on choosing the best residential properties. Real estate investment opportunities that will make you rich.

iUniverse books may be ordered through booksellers or by contacting:

iUniverse
1663 Liberty Drive
Bloomington, IN 47403
www.iuniverse.com
1-800-Authors (1-800-288-4677)

Because of the dynamic nature of the Internet, any web addresses or links contained in this book may have changed since publication and may no longer be valid. The views expressed in this work are solely those of the author and do not necessarily reflect the views of the publisher, and the publisher hereby disclaims any responsibility for them.

Any people depicted in stock imagery provided by Thinkstock are models, and such images are being used for illustrative purposes only. Certain stock imagery © Thinkstock.

ISBN: 978-1-4917-9253-7 (sc)
ISBN: 978-1-4917-9252-0 (e)

Library of Congress Control Number: 2016904791

Print information available on the last page.

iUniverse rev. date: 04/11/2016

Special Note

This book is dedicated to the loving memory of my mother who passed away whilst I was in the midst of writing this book. Not being around her during the final days of her life hurts a lot till this day. Not being able to say a proper good-bye hurts even more. This is the greatest regret of my life.

"Mama, thank you for everything you have sacrificed and done for me during your lifetime. Good-bye and may you rest in eternal peace".

Disclaimer

Disclaimer

"Huge Returns from Property Investments"
Copyright © 2016 – All Rights Reserved

The information included in this book is for educational purposes only and is not meant to be a substitute for seeking the advice of a professional realtor. The author has made all efforts to ensure the information in this book is accurate. However, there are no warranties as to the accuracy or completeness of the contents herein and therefore the author cannot be held responsible for any errors, omissions, or dated material.

This book contains methods and other advice that, regardless of my own results and experience, may not produce the same results (or any results) for you. The author makes absolutely no guarantee, expressed, or implied, that by following the advice, or using the data below, the readers will get the same results, as there are several factors and variables that come into play regarding any given situation.

Liability Disclaimer:

By reading this book, you assume all risks associated with using the advice, data, and suggestions given below, with a full understanding that you, solely, are responsible for anything that may occur as a result of putting this information into action in any way, and regardless of your interpretation of the advice.

You further agree that the author cannot be held responsible in any way for the success or failure of your business as a result of the information presented below. It is your responsibility to conduct your own due diligence regarding the safe and successful operation of your business, if you intend to apply any of my information in any way to your business operations.

What This Book Holds For You

If you are new to the real estate business, there is a lot that you need to learn about it. First of all, real estate business is a great way to earn maximized profit on your investments. The real estate market is not only for the rich but for anyone and everyone who is interested in buying properties and selling them.

This book is dedicated to all the people out there who want to invest in real estate for a minimum of 10% ROI. The good news for such buyers is that they can earn great profits by purchasing the properties I have for them. Real estate can be tricky at times. You will either get an unexpectedly high return on investments or you will go under losses. However, if you are purchasing investment properties from a trusted investor, then you have a greater chance of earning huge ROI. This real estate guide focuses on major areas of your investment journey including:

- Reasons you should invest in real estate.
- Earning ROI by buying properties.
- Tips to earn maximum rent.
- Buying real estate properties with little cash.
- Tips on choosing the best residential properties.
- Real estate investment opportunities that will make you rich.
- Assessing the right investment opportunity.
- Quality advice from a professional.

This book is a complete guide that will enable you to excel in real estate market and help you earn massive ROI. If you want to gain success in real estate business, you need to have the right experience and knowledge. With my knowledge and experience in the real estate business, I can take you to the right path and help you earn easy returns on your investments. Without the help of this book, you will not be able to make the most of your real estate investments. Remember, real

Alex Lee

estate is a risky business and to succeed, you have to create a perfect game plan or simply take help from a professional who has complete knowledge about this business.

Let's proceed with the book and make better real estate decisions.

Good Luck!

Table of Contents

Introduction: Is This Business For You?

When you invest your money in a business, there are always risks attached because you are not certain whether your investments will turn into great returns or just end up getting dissolved. Real estate is one such business that has its fair share of risks. However, real estate investments made after in-depth research are extremely beneficial and result in high return on investments.

This is exactly what this book has in store for you. Before getting into this business, you need to have complete knowledge and it takes several years to get into the game. However, with the help of an expert or an investor, you can make the most of your purchase. When it comes to purchasing investment properties, everyone is looking to earn profit. Whether it is 2% or 5% ROI, when buyers calculate it over the years, they get a great amount of money in their bank accounts, and that's exactly what they want.

When you purchase a property for the first time, you need to be very careful in creating strategies for earning massive returns. If you have ample knowledge of the different markets, you will be able to buy homes at lowest price and sell them at maximum. Real estate investments are a gamble. You never know when the market goes down and when it goes up. However, you can use your knowledge to predict the market or simply take help of a realtor to avoid making a risky investment.

There are many people who have a great financial back-up but do not have adequate knowledge about real estate investments. Such people need support from experienced buyers and that's exactly the value at offer.

As a real estate investor for quite some time, I have realized that it is really challenging to look for the perfect property in a great neighborhood that has the potential to sell at incredible rates. The time that I have spent working with different investors, buyers, sellers, and realtors has given me the aptness to make sound decisions. Buying properties isn't all that simple after all. When you are buying a property, you have to dig deep into the details. You have to see whether the property is in the right location or not. You also need to make sure that you get it inspected before putting your money in it. Therefore, it is best to buy properties from an experienced real estate investor, who has the knowledge and expertise to put the best properties on offer for their customers. The main goal for every investor should be to buy properties that have the potential to be sold out at much higher rate. Your real estate investments should be able to create a flowing income for investors. Once you buy your first property, you need to decide whether you want to sell it or put it up for rent. The decision you make relies on the market conditions. If the property value is seeing an all time high, it is best to sell it and if the property value is going down, you can put it up for rent and earn money every month.

Chapter 1: Reasons To Get In The Real Estate Business

The real estate business is one of the best businesses to invest in. The reason that the opportunities in this business never come to an end is that everyone needs a home to live in. As the population increases, the demand in purchasing real estate also increases.

The best thing about investing in real estate is that you get to enjoy a lot of profit on properties that you bought when the market value was down. If you are really looking to earn maximum profit on your investment, then this business is right for you. Let me tell you why you need to invest in real estate.

Increased Value Over Time

How often do you come across a business opportunity that increases in value with passing time? Well, real estate market is full of benefits for the investor. Whether you plan to sell your properties or keep them with you for a longer time, you will see its value appreciating. This happens due to the development and growth in communities which create greater chances for real estate investors to sell their properties. The concept is simple; the longer you keep the property with you, the higher will be the return. This appreciation in value is due to the increase in demand. So, we all are well aware that the population continues to grow and with it grows opportunities for real estate investors.

Increased Leverage

I have come across many people who tell me that they are not right for the real estate business because they don't have a massive bank balance.

It might be easier to buy properties with lots of money in your account but it is certainly not the only way you can enter this business.

The thing that I admire about real estate business is that it has so many opportunities for everyone. Even if you don't have a lot of money to invest in a property right away, you can go for different options. Real estate business offers opportunities for borrowing. If you don't have enough investments, you can get a loan from a bank. The reason that banks easily give loans for real estate investments is that it is a tangible asset. Moreover, the overall returns from this asset are higher, which makes it appealing to the banks as well.

Greater Tax Deductions

Owning any other business might result in increased taxes but investing in real estate is nothing like that. When you invest in real estate, you can claim deductions on a number of things including repairs, maintenance, insurance, traveling for business purposes, interest paid on the loan, building depreciation, and agent's fee.

Real estate investments are also good for getting interest on mortgage payments deducted. This allows investors to save money on taxes.

Complete Ownership

What is so great about this business is that you are the one and only owner of it. You have complete control of your properties and you can handle all the tasks related to your properties on your own. Whether it is rent collection or mortgage payments, you are responsible for it all.

When you look at other investment opportunities like stocks, you cannot handle the trades on your own, and require a broker to help you with it. Greater control means that you do not have to worry about anyone trying to cheat you, which is usually the case with businesses where there are several departments and managers. In the real estate business, you are your own manager and you can do whatever you like with your investment properties.

Long-Term Investment

Everyone wants to invest in an asset that they can benefit from in the long-run. The most valuable asset that people can invest in is real estate properties. You can also choose to put the property up for rent and earn flowing cash for as long as you own the property.

Having real estate properties simply means that you have something that you can take advantage of in the future. The best thing is that the value of real estate properties is under a constant change. This means that even when you buy a property when the market rates are lower, you will be able to sell it at a much higher rate when the market value is high. Therefore, investing in real estate should earn you massive profits.

Get to Make Renovations

You cannot just have a property and not be able to benefit from it. The reason that I simply love this business is that it gives me a lot of control. A real estate property is a tangible asset and when you know that you are the boss, you can do anything with it.

If you believe that real estate investments are risky, then you will be pleased to find out that your property's value is in your own hands. Because you are the owner, you can make significant changes to the property to make it look more appealing.

This is a technique many investors are implementing with the properties that are not very valuable. You can remodel your property to turn it into a modern home and put it up for rent. If there are issues with a property, you can make necessary fixtures without having to ask anyone. This way, you can increase the value of your property even if the market is seeing a low.

Flexible Price

When you invest in stocks, you know you cannot sell it for a penny more or less. You can only sell it at the current market price. However, that's not the case with real estate investments. When you invest in a property, you are its legal owner and you can sell it at a price that you find suitable.

In the real estate business, you have the opportunity to negotiate the rates based on the property you have. You can also hire a representative or a realtor to negotiate the price of the home and sell it for a price higher than the market rates. It is all about selling in this business. Buying properties from an experienced investor should be risk-free. The investors that you buy properties from should have the most attractive properties at offer. These are the properties that have a potential to be sold out at a much higher rate, making it a win-win situation for me and my customers.

The Safest Option

Investing in real estate business is a great way to maximize on profits. There are just too many benefits of investing in this business that it is really hard to keep away from it. However, real estate can be tricky and unless you are a professional, you will incur losses in terms of the types of properties you buy and the area you pick.

Although there are risks in the real estate business, there is another great way to minimize these risks. In order to play safe, especially if you are new to the business, you should buy properties from an investor like me. Big investors buy many properties based on their experience and knowledge of the market. They offer these properties to other investors at good rates. The reason buying from an investor is that they are highly experienced and can offer the best deal on good properties.

This makes it easy for anyone interested in this business to invest in properties without worrying about the market and the property type. This gives people a great chance to make the most of their investments without worrying about losses.

Chapter 2: Types Of Properties You Can Buy

Have you ever wondered what is so great about real estate business that everyone wants to get into it? Well, it isn't too hard to explain that.

The reason that the real estate business is so popular among investors is that they get to enjoy its many benefits. Due to the opportunities this business holds, it is almost impossible for anyone to stay away from it. Another great thing about the real estate business is that it has a lot of options for the investors. There are several types of properties that investors can buy based on their interest and the market that they want to serve.

With so many options at hand, investors can choose to specialize in one type of property or buy all types of properties. I sell a pretty dynamic range of properties myself. These properties are carefully picked and inspected, and then put up for sale. Let's take a look at the different types of properties that you can buy.

Plain Land

Plain land or farmland is a land that doesn't have a building or a home built on it. It might be the last option that investors would go for but it is extremely beneficial in a number of ways. Firstly, the thing that investors need to understand that investing in such types of properties is very different than investing in a home. Because when you invest in a home, you plan to live in it, you cannot do so with a plain land. Another thing that investors need to know is that you cannot get tax deductions on a plain land like you could in a residential or commercial property.

However, farmlands are still very attractive to investors who want to diversify their market portfolio. Another great thing about investing in a farmland is that it is always in demand. Although a farmland is different than a plain land in many ways, it still brings a lot for opportunities for investors. Let's take a look at some of the benefits of investing in vacant land that will definitely make you consider this option.

➢ Selling to Other Investors

What do we invest in properties for? Yes, to sell them to earn profit. Similarly, when you invest in a vacant land, you can earn great returns by selling it. A vacant land might seem less attractive to you but there are many investors who need a land to build a private property on it. You might not get as many investors for it but you will get just enough to sell it at a good price.

There are many people who are looking for vacant lands in order to build a custom home, an office building, or simply use the land for business purposes. This is the segment of the market that you can really attract in order to sell your property.

➢ Sub-dividing the Property

Another great way to earn great returns on vacant land is to subdivide the property. This option is best for those who don't want to sell their entire land. This option is also more beneficial as it allows land owners to make the most of market rates and keep some portions of the land to themselves for maximum return. Subdividing the land and selling small portions of it is extremely profitable, and it enables investors to earn and still have more portions to sell.

➢ Building a Home on the Land

The best way to earn massively from vacant land is to build on it. However, you need to make sure that you have double checked every law and construction rules before starting onto the process. Once you are able to get construction permission, you can make the most of your investment.

It is obviously an expensive option to construct a new building from scratch, but once you have the final product in front of you, you can attract a lot of investors. If the land that you bought is huge in size, you can subdivide it and construct small homes on different portions. This is also a great way to make the most of your initial investment and get maximized returns.

➢ A Vacant Land is Risk Free

Good news for those investors who are afraid of investing in real estate because of the last recession is that the value of a vacant land doesn't depreciate. Because the value of vacant lands constantly rises, they do not get affected by inflation.

➢ Great Long-Term Investment

Investing in a vacant land means that you can benefit from it in the long term. Even if you are not planning on selling the land, you can keep it as a tangible asset.

➢ Costs Less

One of the best things about investing in a vacant land is that it costs much less than a completely constructed property. Because a vacant land is not developed, it is more affordable for an investor who is new in the business. Another reason for its affordability is that a vacant land doesn't require maintenance like developed properties. You also get to save some money on taxes.

➢ Used for Farming Purposes

If you want to earn a flowing income out of your vacant land, it is best to put the land up for rent for farming. When the land will be used for business purposes, you will not only be able to earn money on rent but you will also be able to get a slight profit margin from the farming activities being performed on your land. What makes vacant lands perfect for investment is that they offer flexibility. Once you buy the land, you are its rightful owner and you can choose to use it anyway you want (of course you cannot use it for any illegal purpose).

Single Family Homes

Single family homes are considered to be one of the most liquid real estate investments. When picking a property to invest in, there are a number of factors that you need to consider including market conditions, location of the property, and its condition. However, if you are looking for immediate returns, then investing in a single family home is the best way to go. Let's find out why you should invest in single family homes.

➤ *Sold in a Shorter Period of Time*

When you invest in a single family home, you get a chance to sell it in a shorter period of time than any other type of investment property. The reason that these properties sell quicker is that there is a high demand for small homes in the market. Because single family homes are more affordable, they are the first choice for many families.

➤ *Easy to Rent*

The thing that makes single family home so attractive is that they have fewer rent limitations. When people are looking for a manageable size place to live, they often look for two options; condos and single family homes.

The reason that many tenants do not like to pick condos is that their rent is too high. Although the rent of a condo includes a variety of service and maintenance fee, it is still more expensive than a single family home.

Tenants believe that the extra fee that they pay for services like garbage disposal, cleaning, mowing, etc is unnecessary because they can do these chores themselves. Therefore, paying extra money for these services doesn't make sense to them, and they want to pick something that is more affordable. That's the reason people usually look for single family homes as they are more affordable than condos and you do not have to pay extra money for things that you can do on your own.

Single family homes are just like condos. Both types of properties offer the same value, the same quality, and the same size. So, tenants do not want to pay extra for something that they can get at a lower price. So, when you invest in single family homes, you know that you have greater opportunities. You can invest in multiple single family homes and put them up for rent to earn massive.

➢ Great Financial Benefits

One of the best things about investing in single family homes is that they have lower interest rates. Another great thing about this type of property is that they have higher loan to value ratios.

➢ Higher Appreciation

When it comes to single family homes, their value is determined based on location and lifestyle. It is all about picking the right type of property and if you are buying from a trustworthy investor, then you should be able to relax as all of the single family homes that you will buy from them will be in great locations. The homes that good investors offer to their clients promote a good lifestyle, which is one of the primary reasons that people purchase or rent a home.

So, if you have bought a single family home that is in a great location, you can see its value going up over time.

➢ Decreased Property Taxes and Insurance Rates

Single family homes save a lot of costs. These homes have lower insurance rates and because they come under residential properties, the taxes on them are lower. Investing in a single family home means that you do not have to pay for commercial property taxes. This is a great way to save costs and make the most out of your investment.

Multi-Family Homes

If you are in the mood to invest massive in the real estate business, then I would suggest that you go for multi-family homes. Multi-family homes are perfect for earning maximum returns on your investment. This type of investment means that you will be buying multiple homes under one roof. Let's take a look at some other benefits that will make you believe that investing in multi-family homes is the most profitable.

➢ *Greater Cash Flow*

The first and the most attractive thing about investing in multi-family homes is that you get to put multiple properties on rent. Once you start earning a flowing income through rent on a monthly basis, you will want to invest in more multi-family homes. However, if you want to rent all of your homes, you have to make sure that the location is ideal.

➢ *Lower Risk*

One of the most major concerns for investors is that they do not want to buy a risky property. If you are one of them, you need to invest in multi-family homes.

When you invest in a single family home, you have one source of income which comes through the rent that the tenant pays. In case you lose the tenant, you have 0% income. However, when you have multiple homes, you have multiple tenants paying you rent. So, even if one tenant leaves you, you have others that pay rent to you every month.

This is what makes multi-family homes so attractive. They are risk free and provide a flowing income.

➢ *Favorable Economies of Scale*

Let's say you purchase four single family homes that you have to manage separately. You have to look after every home and keep it maintained. The more homes you have, the greater will be your responsibility and costs. However, when you invest in multi-family homes, you have multiple tenants living under one roof. This means that you have less responsibility and fewer things to manage. This is definitely in your favor as investing in multi-family homes provide favorable economies of scale for the investors.

➢ *Easy to Manage Tenants*

The cash flow from multi-family homes is huge, which means that you have a chance to hire a management company to manage your tenants. It can be really hard to look after multiple tenants and to ensure that everyone pays rent on time. A management company on the other hand will look after every matter and keep you relaxed.

➢ *Great Tax Benefits*

There are so many pros of investing in multi-family homes that buyers definitely need to consider putting their money in them. Another great benefit of investing in multi-family homes is that you get to enjoy tax breaks.

When you own multi-family homes in a good community, you are doing a good thing for the people by providing them homes to live in. This is what the government aims to do, and that's the reason you can easily enjoy tax incentives from the government.

As owning multi-family homes and putting them up for rent means that you are running a business, this gives you a great opportunity to take several deductions on tasks related to your business. In order to make the most of these tax benefits, you can hire a CPA to help you with it. Because you are earning massive income every month, you can easily afford a CPA.

Commercial Properties

When it comes to investing in real estate, not many people consider buying commercial properties. Commercial properties might require a greater investment but they are much more profitable. The world's wealthiest real estate investors like Donald Trump make their money off of commercial investments. Commercial real estate is packed with perks for an investor. Even when the economy goes down, these properties help provide you with a flowing income. Commercial real estate includes retail stores, office buildings, and industrial complexes. Due to the expanding economy, there will always be a demand of renting office spaces or business outlets, so you will never be out of tenants.

There is no doubt that commercial real estate is less risky than any other type of real estate investment. Whether the market is down or not, a commercial real estate investor gets to enjoy a variety of perks. Read on to find out why investing in commercial properties is a good choice.

➤ Low Vacancy Ratio

Commercial properties are the types of properties that include office spaces that consist of multiple units. Because these properties are multi-unit, they have a very low risk of vacancy. Let's say you own a commercial property that has twenty units. You put all the units on rent and only one unit remains vacant. This means that you just have 5% vacancy, which is not bad given that you are already getting rent for nineteen units. This makes commercial properties way more attractive than any other type of real estate investment.

➤ Rock Solid Income

The best thing about investing in commercial real estate is that it allows you to earn massive income. Commercial properties are secured by a lease agreement, which is the reason an investor can earn a higher income. Because commercial properties are meant for businesses, the rent which an investor gets out of them is much higher. The income that an investor earns out of commercial real estate is much higher than single-family homes, multi-family homes, and apartments. This makes commercial properties more attractive than any other type of real estate.

➤ Lots of Allowances

When it comes to allowances, commercial properties offer a lot of perks. A commercial property owner can get relief and cost cuts on air conditioning, lighting, carpets, and plant equipment. These allowances and cost cuts will allow commercial real estate investors to enjoy maximum income with added benefits.

➤ *Greater Freedom*

Commercial properties also offer greater freedom to owners who can choose to make desired changes to their properties. Commercial property owners can make major decisions for their properties including renovations, change of tenants, development, and the terms of lease. This gives investors a chance to have greater control over their property.

➤ *Serious Buying Offers*

Commercial real estate is meant for businesses and that's the reason the buyers and renters discuss the rates seriously. When you look at residential properties, buyers often try to use an emotional appeal with the sellers in order to get a better deal. However, when businesses deal with commercial real estate investors, the discussion is very formal in nature. Both parties are aware that it is a business and they need to respect what the other has to offer. Although buyers have room to negotiate, they are still easier to convince than residential buyers.

There are many other benefits to commercial real estate that are enough to convince you to get into this business. Commercial real estate investments allow you to earn massively and enjoy the appreciation of value on the property for several years.

Types of Commercial Real Estate Investment Properties

Now that we are well aware of the perks that investing in commercial real estate offers, we need to learn about the different types of properties that one can choose to invest in based on their value. Let's continue reading.

➤ *Land*

Did you know that the value of a commercial property is calculated based on the land and the development over it?

Investing in a plain commercial land is packed with benefits but it is also really hard to find a land to invest in. Because plain lands are rare, investing in it means you should have a great amount of money. Due to their scarcity, plain lands are sold at much higher rates.

Moreover, if you develop a building over this land, you can earn a lot more. That's the reason it is extremely important to invest in properties and lands from a reputable investor that has carefully picked the best properties. This means that investing in a land has a great potential for making investors earn maximum profit.

➤ *Office Buildings*

Office buildings are the type of commercial real estate that offers a lot of benefits. These buildings include several units, which means that you will be able to earn a flowing income. Because these units are leased by businessmen for their office space, their lease lasts for a longer period of time. Many businesses rent office buildings for a time period of three to four years, which gives you a great chance to earn a regular income without any break. Moreover, due to a high demand in office spaces, there is a little chance of vacancy. Even if all of your units are not rented, you still earn a flowing income from other tenants.

➤ *Retail Stores*

Retail stores do not require a huge investment like office buildings or land. You can simply invest in one or two retail stores to put them up for rent. However, if you really want to earn maximum profit through a retail store investment, you need to make sure that your property is at a good location.

The key to earning great returns on retail stores is to choose an attractive location. A good location is one which is in a highly crowded place. If your store is in a high traffic area, you can easily ask for a higher rent. If a tenant knows that having this store will give their business an edge over others, they will be willing to pay a higher rent for it.

Although commercial real estate investment is of greater value than residential properties, there is still a lot one has to look into before making such a huge investment. When investing in commercial real estate, there are certain things that you need to keep in mind like the location and the building. Having a commercial property in a poor location will not do you any good. Therefore, it is best to buy commercial properties from an experienced investor who carefully picks out properties in a good location. The value of a commercial property mostly depends on its location. This means that if the property is in a good location, you get to maximize your profits.

Chapter 3: Importance Of Inspecting The Property

Real estate investment is not just about buying, selling, and renting but a great part of this business depends upon how well you take care of your properties. Property inspection is a must if you are looking to earn great returns on your investment.

Although you need to be very careful when choosing a property to invest, you will still need to get it examined in order to make sure that everything is in perfect shape. When you are aiming at a good cash flow, you need to be pro-active in keeping the property well-maintained. The first thing that buyers look at in a property is its condition. They inspect the property inside out to ensure that nothing is damaged. If they find something that needs repair, they will ask the owners to get it fixed, which means unanticipated costs. If you want to avoid paying for repairs and renovation at the time of selling, you need to make sure that the property is well-maintained.

Let's look at some reasons which will help you learn about the importance of home inspection.

No Chance of Renegotiations

When it comes to buying a house, people are very choosy and particular. When you are selling a home that is in a perfect shape, you do not have to worry about buyers knocking on your door for a renegotiation of the price. However, when you sell a faulty property to a buyer, there is a high chance that the buyer will return to you for negotiating the deal all over again. In such cases, either the buyer asks for a lower price to cover the costs of repairs or maintenance or they ask for the problems to be fixed, which means sellers need to invest more money into the property. Either way, if you are trying to sell a poorly maintained property, chances are that you will incur a loss.

17

Therefore, it is best to inspect the property before putting it up for sale. A well maintained property is most likely to sell at a good price without leading to any renegotiations.

A Good Return on Investment

If you think that investing in property inspection is a waste of money, then you are sadly mistaken. When you get your property thoroughly inspected, you are able to fix any problems in it. This results in a well-maintained and attractive property that will attract several potential buyers. When you deal with all the issues prior to selling the property, you are able to sell it quicker.

Buyers are in search of properties that provide good value on their money. Therefore, a well maintained property is at the top of their priority list and when they come across such a property, they are ready to purchase it at a good price. A well-preserved property can be sold at a handsome price without many of negotiations. So, investing in property inspection is only going to reward you at the time of sale.

Quote a Higher Price for Your Property

Another great perk of getting your property inspected is that you can ask for an increased price for it. Buyers do not like to manage inspections, repairs, and maintenance on their own because it is a costly job and requires a lot of time. However, when a property is already maintained by the seller, it is easier to sell it at a higher price.

Sellers can simply ask for a higher price for the property when they have invested in home inspection and maintenance. They can make it a solid point with the buyers and earn maximum profit. When the buyers know that the property is well-sustained, they will more likely agree to pay the higher quoted price.

Build Trust within Buyers

When you get a property inspected, you can present a pre-inspection report to the buyers to give them a point to trust you. This report will help buyers have trust in you that you are not hiding anything from them. This is a great way to increase your credibility and build trust within buyers, and increase your chances of attracting more buyers for your properties. Offering free service like this will allow you to quote a higher price for the property, which buyers are more likely to agree upon.

Peace of Mind

Inspecting a property for damages before putting it up for sale simply means that you are offering the best thing to the buyers. However, when you sell a property that has problems in its systems and needs maintenance, you know that you are cheating on buyers by selling them poorly maintained property. In order to enjoy that peace of mind, you should get a property inspected before you are ready to sell it. This will give you relief that you are honest with your buyers.

Another major reason for getting a property inspected before you sell it is to avoid bad buyer reactions and actions. Many buyers expect the sellers to sell a property that is already inspected and when they find out that it needs a lot of work, they get furious and are more likely to opt-out of buying the property. These scenarios are pretty common and can lead to a bad reputation in the market. However, when you sell a properly managed and maintained property, you know that the buyers won't abandon the purchase or break the deal.

Increased Credibility

People in the real estate business are aware that having a good reputation in the market is extremely important to get hold of potential buyers and earn great profits. In order to build reputation and a solid place in the market, real estate investors need to take care of property inspection before selling them.

When you invest in property inspection to fix any problems in the structure and systems of the house, you are automatically increasing your value in the market. The properties that are handled by responsible sellers are the ones that have the potential to sell at higher rates. So, when you sell well-sustained properties, you build credibility in the market. This helps you earn respect and trust from the realtors and buyers, making it easier for you to be successful in this business.

Tips for Property Inspection

As a real estate investor, you should pay extra attention to your property, especially its maintenance. Selling a property is not just about getting rid of it to earn profit but it is also about maximizing your total investment on the property. When you put up your property on the market, you attract many buyers. Because buying properties is a huge decision and people are price sensitive, they conduct thorough research and inspection before putting their money into them. Buyers usually look at every corner of a property to ensure that it is well taken care of and doesn't require any major investments.

In order to make your properties sell at a good rate, you need to think about getting the property inspected. Of course, if you have bought your investment property from a trusted seller, you don't have to worry about inspections. However, when the property is with you for several months, you will need to take responsibility of its inspection for increasing your chances at earning massive profit. Let's take a look at some tips which will help you keep your property in top shape.

Hire a Property Inspection Company

The easiest way to get a property inspected is to hire a property inspection company. Property inspection companies have the right experience and expertise to thoroughly inspect and fix the problems in a property. For a property seller, it is important to ensure that the property is in perfect shape before it is ready to be visited by buyers. Although property inspection can be done by the seller itself, it is best to leave the job to a professional who has a better idea of properties.

Property inspectors are able to address minor issues that can turn into huge problems over the time. They conduct preventative maintenance to in all parts of the property to ensure that everything is working in perfect condition. It is best to hire a property inspection company when you have owned the property for several months. Home inspectors are experts who know their work very well. So, when you call a home inspector to look at your property, they will check every corner of the property to make sure nothing is damaged. Even if you are unable to identify the root cause of a problem, a property inspector will help you with it. They are also very helpful in suggesting possible repairs and solutions to fix a problem.

Property inspectors are not only helpful in pointing out problems in the house but they are also helpful in inspecting a repair. If you recently had a repair made to your property, you can ask a property inspector to examine it. Property inspectors will examine the repair closely and will tell you whether the job was done properly or not. This is a great way of keeping a check on home repairs and renovation projects before you put your property up for sale.

Conducting Property Inspection on Your Own

Many sellers who do not want to spend money on hiring a home inspector often take the job upon themselves. Property inspection is not rocket science and many people are able to do it on their own. However, in order to make the right decisions, you need to have experience working with home repairs and maintenance.

When you are conducting inspection on your own, you need to carefully observe the places that are most vulnerable to damage. You also need to take a close look at the different systems of the house to find damage.

Things You Will Need

When you start inspecting your property, you will need to make sure you have the right tools to get the job done. To conduct proper property inspection, you will need the following tools:

➢ Pair of Gloves
➢ Flashlight

These things are a must to take along when going for a property inspection.

What You Need to Inspect

Before deciding to sell your property, you need to make several visits to the property to look for any damage or issue that can turn its value down. Your main aim as a real estate investor is to offer the most valuable and highly maintained properties to the buyers.

When you have taken the responsibility of inspecting the property on your own, you need to make sure you know the exact things to inspect. It is extremely important to give extra attention to the areas that have been renovated or recently repaired. Here is a list of things and areas that you need to give extra attention to when inspecting your property:

➢ Look for holes in the walls or wood using a torch. Holes and opening are often termite spots that are a major problem for homeowners and can cause a home's price to fall.
➢ Inspect the heating and cooling systems in your property to ensure that there is no fault in them. Problems in heating and cooling systems may cost buyers a lot of money. Many buyers also reach out to sellers to ask for repairs to be made, which costs sellers their reputation. Therefore, it is important to carefully examine the HVACS and heaters before selling the home. Test the HVACS and heaters in advance to see whether there is a problem or not.
➢ Carefully inspect the roof of the home that you are about to sell. If there are water stains, cracks, or mould on the roof, then you need to get it fixed immediately. If a problem in a roof is not addressed, it is highly likely that you will need to replace it with a new one. To avoid paying for such a huge cost, try to fix the problem before the damage is beyond repair.
➢ You will also need to pay close attention to the foundation of your property. Observe the ground closely to find big cracks in it. Walk around the property and if you hear unusual sounds coming from the foundation, then you need to get it fixed. Selling a house with cracked floors is not good for your reputation.
➢ One of the first things that buyers see in a property is its exterior. If the house has faded paint and cracked wood, then there is a high chance that buyers won't be interested in entering the house. In order to avoid losing potential buyers, you need to make sure that the exterior of your property is well-maintained. You need to pay

close attention to the paint on the exterior walls and examine the wall for any cracks and holes. It is best to get a fresh paint-job done before putting your house up for sale.

➤ Home insulation has a great impact on energy bills and the effectiveness of heating and cooling systems in a home. Therefore, buyers are very particular about examining a home's windows and doors closely to look for leaks and crack that result in poor insulation and increased energy bills. In order to increase the chances of selling your property at a good price, you need to check the windows and doors carefully. If the windows are cracked or damaged, replace them with new ones. Do not think about the price as replacing the windows is only going to make your home look attractive.

➤ Plumbing systems often incur damage, especially in old properties. Therefore, inspect the different faucets, drains, and pipes in your property to find leaks or damage. A damaged plumbing system can drop your property's value greatly. So, it is best to replace old pipes with new ones and get the faucets fixed.

➤ Interior paint also needs to be fixed, especially if there are water or dirt stains all over it. Take a look at the interior walls and if the paint is making the home look untidy, get a new paint-job done. If wallpaper looks damaged, get it removed.

➤ There are many other changes and fixtures that you will need to make in a property before putting it up for sale including door knobs, lighting, shelves, cabinets, flooring, and ceiling fans.

When you are planning to sell a home to earn great returns, you need to make sure that you have carefully examined the entire property to make necessary changes to it. When making repairs and renovations to your property, do not think about the money that you are investing in it, think about the return that you will get out of it.

The properties that are renovated prior to sale often help attract more buyers, resulting in great returns. So, the investment you make in repairing and maintaining the property will pay off in the form of profits earned from selling or renting the property.

Making a Smart Decision

If you are ready to invest in real estate to sell or rent properties, then you need to buy properties that are sold by trusted realtors or investors. Property maintenance is a huge responsibility that many sellers are not ready to take. If you are one of those sellers who want to get hold of properties that are already well-maintained, then you should look for investors that are offering preserved properties. This is a good way to avoid investing a lot of time, money, and efforts into maintenance, repairs, and renovations.

It is not always that you get an inspection report when you buy a property, but if the home has a ready tenant; you can rest assured that the home is in perfect shape and ready to be bought. Sometimes a perfect property also has minor issues which are easily manageable and can be fixed by buyers on their own. In such cases, you can buy the property and fix the minor issues yourself. However, if there are huge defects and problems in the property that require maintenance, you can consider looking for other houses.

Chapter 4: The Importance Of Property Management

When you are in the real estate business, your main aim is to earn maximum returns on your investments by finding ways to increase the value of your property in the market. Investing in a property isn't only about paying for it but to keep it well-maintained to earn great profits. Property management is one such thing that every real estate investor has to consider in order to attract a greater number of potential tenants and buyers.

When it comes to property management, a person who has only one or two houses to look after can manage the responsibility on their own. However, the investors that have multiple properties and tenants to manage have to consider hiring a property management company to cut costs, save time, and reduce stress. If you are looking to increase the value of your purchased properties, you need to manage the property in the most efficient way. Let's take a look at the importance and benefits of good property management, and how it can prove beneficial for the investors in the long run.

Benefits of Property Management

Property management is an important aspect of the real estate business that every investor needs to consider. When you have multiple properties at hand and you are looking to sell or rent them for maximum profit, you need to ensure that you are doing your best in keeping the property in top shape and managing it in the right way. It is best to get in touch with a property management company that can help you keep organized for maximum benefits. Let's take a look at some benefits that property managers provide to real estate investors.

Hassle-Free Rent Collection

If you are a real estate investor or know anything about real estate business, you would know that collecting rent from tenants can be a challenging task, especially when you have several of them. When rent is not collected on time, it can mean poor cash flow, resulting in failures. That's the reason managing properties is extremely important and if you have hired a property management company, you can relax as the manager will collect rent from every tenant in a systematic order. On-time rent payments are crucial for success in the real estate business and managing it for smooth cash flow can mean great success.

Strict Tenant Screening

A property manager also helps pick the best tenants for your homes. They carefully conduct a background check for every tenant and ensure that every tenant fills out an application with all their details and photo for identification. In order to avoid accepting tenant with a bad track record, property managers check their social security number, any criminal activity in the past, and look for any major cases against them. They also double check the information given in the application to ensure that the tenant is not hiding anything. Property managers will also contact every applicant's previous landlord and employers to learn more about them. This information allows property managers to pick only the most suitable tenants for your properties.

Local Rental Knowledge

Property managers are active part of the real estate market and have complete knowledge about current local rental rates. They also make use of the Internet to look at the rental rates offered by different landlords in order to come up with the best rate for your property. Property managers have extensive experience in the real estate business. They are aware that tenants can research about different properties and their rents easily on the Internet and choose the property that has the lowest rent. This knowledge allows property managers to quote a price that is attractive for the tenants and as a result helps provide you with greater cash flow.

Complete Knowledge of Property Laws and Regulations

When you are managing your properties on your own, there is a high chance that you miss out on one or two property laws and regulations. When you do not have extensive knowledge about properties and their law, you often end up making mistakes and paying penalties. However, when you have a property manager by your side, you can relax as they are experienced in their field and are up-to-date with the latest property laws and regulations. They make every decision keeping laws first, which is why you do not end up breaking any rules or regulations. Property managers keep a check on local, state, and federal rules to ensure that your investment is safe.

Experienced Marketers

If you own properties and want to sell them or put them up for rent, you would know the amount of time it takes to attract great buyers and tenants. However, a property manager has expertise in marketing real estate properties for attracting potential buyers to get you the best deal. Property managers also make use of different online and offline marketing tactics to look for tenants and buyers as quickly as possible. They know how to market a property in the best possible way. With the help of their marketing knowledge, property managers are able to avoid keeping your properties vacant for long times, which helps save lots of costs.

Responsible Routine Inspections

When you own properties for rent or selling purpose, you know it is extremely important to keep them in top shape. In order to get the best deal on your properties, your properties should be well maintained and carefully looked after. If you are handling your properties on your own, it will be really hectic to conduct inspection of each one of them. However, a property management company handles property inspections professionally. Many property management companies conduct routine inspections twice every year. These inspections aren't only for preparing homes for sale or rent, but they are conducted even after tenancy.

If you are looking to attract more people to your properties and earn a good return on them, you can take advantage of property managers that help manage properties in a routinely manner. Property managers also prepare inspection reports to help increase the value of your properties. When tenants have a complaint against an issue in the property that needs maintenance, property managers are the ones to handle it. Having property managers will keep you relaxed as your property will be kept well-maintained without you having to stress over anything.

Great Connections in the Market

Property management companies have great relationships and connections with vendors, contractors, and suppliers. Their special skills and professionalism helps real estate investors make the best choice when it comes to taking decisions regarding property maintenance or upgrade. They also have extensive knowledge and experience which enable them to choose the most reliable workers for a project or task. They also get the most affordable rates from contractors, helping you save money.

Due to the reputation and connections of property managers in the market, they are able to increase credibility for investors.

Deal with Emergencies

Dealing with multiple tenants can be quite a nuisance, especially when it comes to dealing with their problems and handling emergency situations. As real estate investors and landlords, you understand that it is important to keep the tenants happy and satisfied. Therefore, you have to address to every issue in a timely manner. Because it is almost impossible to handle complaints and queries of several tenants at a time, you can take help from a property manager.

A property manager will communicate with all the tenants via text messages, emails, and calls. They will be available to the tenants 24/7, helping solve their problems and emergency situations in a timely manner.

Higher Tenant Retention Rates

When you keep tenants happy and satisfied, you increase the chances of making them stay for longer. Property managers make use of smart tactics to enhance customer experience that results in improved occupancy rate. Property managers set up portals to make it easier for tenants to contact them. They create ways to make it easier and convenient for tenants to pay their rent. They also improve the safety and appearance of the community to ensure that tenants are willing to stay for a long time.

Improved Communication

Property managers also help bridge the communication gap between tenants and landlords, helping form better relations. These managers often serve as middle-men, helping tenants and landlords communicate with one another. Property managers also make notes of tenants' complaints and deliver them to the landlords. When it is time to increase the rent, these property managers help move the process smoothly. Due to their effective communication skills, these managers help make rent collection process quite simple.

Major Cost Savings

Having a property manager by your side means that you will be saving on a lot of costs. Because property managers are experienced and have a vast network, they are able to get the best rates on different business operations and property maintenance projects. Although property managers handle an array of chores, they charge around 6% to 10% of the monthly rent collected. This means that your properties get managed at a lower price, helping you earn maximum profit.

When you are in the real estate business, you want to earn huge ROI. In order to earn a smooth cash flow, you should consider hiring a property manager to handle all the time consuming tasks so that you have time to focus on money making strategies for expanding your real estate business.

Picking the Best Property Management Company

When looking for a property management company that is best for you, you need consider a variety of factors. In order to make the most of a property manager, make sure you pick the best one by conducting an in-depth research and asking relevant questions. Read onto a list of questions that every investor should ask property managers before hiring them.

What is the cost?

When hiring a property management company, the first thing that you need to look at is their costs. Ask the property managers about the cost that they will charge. Make sure that the costs that they quote are inclusive of all services. Property managers' charge somewhere between 4 to 12 percent of the rent collected. So, make sure that the price is right for you. Do not go for a company that charges separately for every service.

What services are included?

Different property management companies offer different services and to ensure that you are getting the help you need, you need to ask about the services that the company offers. A good company will be the one which will meet your requirements. However, make sure that services like financial management, property maintenance, reports formation, rent collection, property insurance claims, and tax calculations are included in the contract.

What is the experience?

When you are looking for a property management company, it is extremely important to pick the one that has an extensive experience. Before moving on with the final decision, you need to ask the property management company about their experience. Make sure that the company has experience handling properties like yours. Ask to look at their portfolio to ensure that the company handles properties in the most efficient way. You can also ask for references of previous clients to see how the company works.

Who will be taking the responsibility?

Property management companies assign different property managers to different clients. Therefore, it is important to meet the manager in person before sealing the deal. Ask to meet the person who will be handling your properties. Carefully observe the manager to ensure that they are professional and have complete knowledge about property management.

What is the back-up plan?

Do not forget to ask about the back-up plan in case the assigned property manager is not able to work. Make sure that the company has an alternate solution when your property manager is unavailable. Ask to meet the back-up property manager and check to see whether he/she is perfect for the job. If there is no back-up plan in place, do not choose the company as it might cause you trouble in the future.

Do you have any hidden charges?

Apart from the upfront cost mentioned in the contract, some companies charge extra for some chores. Therefore, it is important to find out about those hidden charges before signing the contract in order to avoid any surprises.

How do you handle tenant problems and rent collections?

When hiring a property management company, you need to make sure that it has a proper plan to deal with tenants. Ask the company about their strategy to handle tenant problems, queries, and emergencies. Also make sure to ask them about the rent collection process. In order to ensure that the property manager handles different processes in a professional way, give them a hypothetical scenario and ask for their game plan. This will give you an idea of what to expect from the manager and whether to hire them or not.

How do you handle promotions and marketing?

Property managers are responsible for promoting properties to attract potential buyers and renters. A good property manager allows investors to earn maximum profits through marketing and promotion. Therefore, it is a must to find out about their marketing and advertising strategies. Ask the property manager about the advertising and marketing techniques that they will make use of. Moreover, ask about the costs associated with marketing the properties in order to avoid any surprises.

What is your availability?

Property managers should be available at all times to address tenant issues. Therefore, you need to ask about their working hours to ensure that they are available to help tenants. Moreover, ask the managers how tenants can contact them apart from their office hours. Make sure that the manager has a proper communication system in place for you and the tenants.

Ask as many questions as you can until you are completely satisfied with the answers or until you reach onto a decision. Choosing a property management company requires in-depth research and investigation in order to pick the one that is a perfect fit for your properties. By asking questions, you will get to know the company a little better, which will help you make the best decision.

Chapter 5: Costs Involved In Real Estate Investments

Due to the dynamic range of properties available in the real estate market, it has become quite easy for an average person to invest in them. Real estate business provides great opportunities for growth and attractive returns to the investors. Therefore, an increasing number of people are showing interest in this business. However, many people are unaware of the costs that are involved in a real estate investment and end up making wrong choices.

In order to make the most of your investments, it is best to have a complete knowledge of the costs involved with real estate properties. These costs involve upfront value of the property and other ongoing costs.

Up-Front Costs

When you purchase a real estate property, there are some upfront costs that you have to pay immediately. Many first time investors believe that they just have to pay for mortgage and a little percentage of the total value of the home but when they find out about other expenses, they second guess their decision. In order to avoid situations like these, take a look at the total upfront costs that you will need to pay for an investment property.

Initial Deposit

The cost of initial deposit is something that every investor is prepared for. When you are interested in a property and want to secure the deal on it, you have to pay 10% of the quoted value of the property. However, 10% is the minimum requirement and buyers can choose to pay a higher deposit. The thing to remember is that if you are paying less than 80% of the home's value upfront as a deposit, you will need to pay for mortgage insurance.

Mortgage Insurance

When you are purchasing a property and you decide to pay less than 20% of the total value of the property, then you have to pay mortgage insurance.

Legal Fee

When you buy a property, you have to apply for the transfer of ownership on your name legally. The home ownership transfer is often done by a conveyancer or a solicitor. The cost involved with this legal home ownership transfer usually ranges from $600 to $800.

Utilities and Connections

After purchasing a property, you need to make sure that there it has all the connections for utilities and other services before you put it up for sale or rent. You will need to pay for the installation of these utilities and services to make your property ready to be sold or rented.

Stamp Duty

In case you have borrowed a loan from a lender to buy the property, you will need to pay tax on it. This tax is known as stamp duty and its value depends on the amount borrowed for purchasing the property.

On-Going Costs

Apart from the upfront costs involved with real estate investments, there are a few ongoing costs that every investor needs to keep in mind. The purpose of defining these costs is not to scare the investors but to help them stay prepared. When it comes to ongoing costs, one can never come up with an estimate amount as these costs change on a monthly basis. Sometimes these ongoing costs increase while other times they significantly drop.

Building and Landlord Insurance

When you own a property or properties, it is extremely important to get building and landlord insurance to protect yourself and your property from loss. This insurance is necessary to get protection against any unforeseen events and incidents like flooding and fire. It also covers any damage that tenants have made on the property. You can also take advantage of this insurance to protect against losses when tenants refuse to pay or leave the property before the completion of the agreement.

Mortgage Fees

When you borrow a loan to buy a property, you need to make monthly or yearly payments for it, depending on the contract with your lender. Mortgage payments are negotiable and you can set an amount based on your affordability. These payments are to be made regularly or else you have to pay added interest.

Annual Land/Property Tax

When you purchase a property for investment, you are liable to pay land tax. This tax is to be paid to the government on an annual basis. In order to make the payments, you need to contact your state authority. However, different states have different regulations for applying taxes and in most cases it is applied on the interest earned out of a property/land. This means that if you are conducting a business in the property, which is helping you earn revenue, you have to pay taxes.

Government Taxes

Owning investment properties requires landlords to pay government taxes on an annual basis. However, you can get some taxes deducted by taking help from an accountant or tax attorney. The rates of these taxes differ from state to state. Therefore, it is important to learn about the rates of your specific state.

Owner's Corporation Fees

If your investment property is a town house, a flat, or a shared block, then you will need to pay the owner's corporation fees. These fees are paid on a quarterly basis and are meant for the improvement of the community, property, and the surrounding area. This fee also covers building maintenance and its fee depends on the type and condition of the property.

Mortgage Repayments

Apart from annual mortgage payments, you need to make monthly mortgage repayments. The monthly amount of these payments is decided prior to the mortgage agreement. However, the monthly rate may rise depending on the current interest rate.

Utility Charges

When you invest in a property, your main goal is to keep the property well-maintained and running to attract potential buyers. Therefore, you will need to pay for utility services like sewerage charges and water.

Property Management

Owning a property is a huge responsibility and when you are looking to prep it for maximum returns; you have to consider investing in property management. Whether you manage the properties on your own or hire a property management company, you will need to pay for it.

It is best to hire a property management company and pay a fixed amount of money each month instead of doing all the chores on your own. When handling the property on your own, you will need to spend more money on repairs, maintenance, and marketing.

Repairs and Maintenance Costs

Any property requires a lot of maintenance, which costs money. However, when you conduct maintenance or repair on an investment property, you can ask for tax deductions. In order to make the most of this cost cutting advantage, make sure you talk to a tax advisor before claiming deductions.

Inspection

Property inspection is an essential aspect of the real estate business. Property inspections are meant to help owners keep their properties in perfect shape for greater returns. Investors need to conduct home inspections on an annual or bi-annual basis. A detailed property inspection includes complete interior and exterior monitoring. Investors can opt for property inspection companies that will help them get every issue fixed for enhanced appeal of their property, resulting in higher profits.

If you are planning to invest in real estate, you need to learn the different costs involved with it. Although these costs might seem a lot at the moment, when you get in the process, everything seems to fall into place.

Chapter 6: Taking A Loan To Buy Investment Properties

Real estate has become a massive revenue generating business for many investors due to its quickly appreciating and depreciating value. The real estate market allows anyone to make the most of their money by earning maximum returns. Moreover, due to the dynamic range of options in investments properties, people are interested in this business more than ever before.

The real estate business is no longer for the upper class alone. Today, people from all backgrounds can invest in properties to earn increased profits. People with little money can also think about buying properties for investment. Let's take a look at the different loan options that people with little money can opt for in order to get into the real estate business.

Things you need to consider

With the availability of a variety of financial help, anyone can get a loan to invest in real estate. However, when you do not have a lot of money in your bank account, you need to look for properties that are either up on a foreclosure auction or are located in less posh communities.

Getting a loan might sound simple but you need to consider several factors including the amount that you can afford to repay every month. When you borrow a loan from a lender, you have to sign an agreement to pay a specific payment every month. The greater the loan amount, the higher the monthly payment. Therefore, make sure you pick a property that you can afford to get a loan for. The lenders and banks that offer home loans often have strict criteria. In order to get the desired loan, you need to consider the following factors:

Alex Lee

Bank statements

Applying for a home loan requires extensive paperwork including bank statements and documentation of all of your assets. Even if you have a separate savings account, you will need to give a proof of it to the lenders. Once you provide lenders with your bank statements, they will verify the details to ensure that you have enough cash flow to afford a home loan and make regular monthly payments.

These formalities are a requirement because lenders want to feel safe about their investment by offering you a loan. Your bank statements are a proof that you have enough money to borrow a loan and return it within the given timeframe.

Credit history

When you apply for a home loan, the lenders usually require a proof that you can pay back the amount you are borrowing. Therefore, lenders usually ask borrowers to show them their credit score and history. Lenders also contact banks to find out about your credit history to ensure that they are making a risk-free deal.

Your credit history plays an important role in determining whether you are worthy of getting a loan or not. If you have a poor credit score, chances are that you will not be given any home loan. A good credit score represents that you are a responsible person who pays off their bills on time and that is exactly what lenders need to know. In order to ensure that you can pay-back the loan and make its regular payments, lenders will require you to provide them with your credit score and history.

Proof of Employment

Do you think anyone will risk their money by giving you a loan when you do not have a job? Well, lenders surely don't entertain unemployed borrowers as they are a risk to them. No lender is interested in granting you a home loan when you do not have a flowing income. Therefore, in order to increase your chances of getting a loan, you will need to show a proof of your employment to the lenders. Proof of employment means that you have enough money to pay back your loan and make regular monthly payments. If you work on a side job or have a small business, make sure you provide a proof of that to the lenders as well.

Do not hesitate in providing information about your jobs and businesses to the lenders, as it is only going to make them want to give you the loan. The more cash flow you have, the higher your chances of getting a home loan.

Collateral

When you are applying for a home loan, make sure you are aware of the fact that you will need to keep one of your assets as collateral. However, not every loan requires collateral. So, it is best to pick a loan that doesn't require collateral. If you are sure that you can pay back your loan within the given period, don't hesitate to apply for such a loan. Collateral is again a form of security that lenders require from borrowers. These conditions are applied to loans for the borrowers who are unable to repay their loans and lenders sell out their collateral to get the money that the borrowers owe them. Your home, car, and any other valuable asset come under collateral.

Types of Mortgages you can opt for

One of the most important things to consider before applying for a loan is to compare different types of mortgages available in the market. There are several types of mortgages, each with different conditions. The type of home loan you choose can have a major impact on the amount you repay every month. There are mortgages that come with varied interest rates. If you choose the one that has a high interest rate, you might end up paying a lot more than you borrowed.

Mortgage loans are the safest to opt for. However, a mortgage loan is protected by an asset which can either be your home or your car. This means that unless you pay back the loan that you borrowed, your asset is not really safe. Mortgage loans are installment based loans that require you to pay a fixed amount on a monthly basis. This is the most attractive type of loan as it allows you to make your loan repayments in small amounts every month. There are different types of mortgages that you can opt for when buying a home. When choosing a mortgage plan, you need to look for two things; fees and interest rate. A perfect mortgage plan is the one that is flexible and offer a low interest rate. Let's take a look at the different types of mortgage loans available.

Fixed Rate Mortgage

Fixed rate mortgage is the type of mortgage in which borrowers are required to pay a fixed interest rate on their loan. This type of mortgage is very appealing for home buyers who want to pay fewer interests without getting affected by the market rates. However, when going for fixed rate mortgage, it is best to negotiate a lower interest rate with the lender.

In this type of mortgage, a lender will usually try to apply a higher interest rate but if you negotiate, you might get a good deal. Fixed rate mortgages also offer as flexible repayment plan. You can choose to repay your mortgage in 10, 15, or 30 years. Many people go for 30 years option because it allows them to make little monthly payments. However, if you want to get rid of the burden of a mortgage, it is best to go for a 10 or 15 year plan.

Another great thing about a fixed rate mortgage is that you can calculate the amount of money that you will be paying back every month without worrying about the varying interest rates. So, even if the interest rates spike, you don't have to worry about paying more. On the contrary, a fixed rate mortgage does have its own set of disadvantages. When you choose fixed rate mortgage, you do not get to pay a lower interest rate when the market rates go down.

Choosing a 15 year fixed rate mortgage plan can help you build greater equity in a short span. If you want to get a great deal out of your mortgage plan, then make sure you negotiate on the interest rates with your lender. Because the interest rates are usually higher for fixed rate mortgages, you will need to put forward your best negotiation skills to lower down the interest rate.

Variable Rate Mortgage

Variable rate mortgage is the opposite of fixed rate mortgage. When you choose variable rate mortgage, you will require paying the interest rate that is prevailing in the market. This means that when the interest rates go high, you will need to make higher monthly payments and when the interest rates lower down; you will get to make lower monthly payments.

There are both advantages and disadvantages attached to this type of mortgage plan. The good thing about this plan is that when the interest rates go down, you get to save a lot of money. However, there will be times when the interest rates will be very high and you will need to pay a greater amount of money to your lenders. For some borrowers, variable rate might be a feasible option but for someone who doesn't want to take the risk, this mortgage is not suitable at all.

A variable rate mortgage is also not suitable for people who like to pre-plan their monthly payments. Because the interest rates vary throughout the mortgage plan, it becomes really hard to calculate the costs over the years. Variable rate mortgages are further divided into several sub-categories that we will discuss below.

One Year VRM Plan

The one year VRM plan is the one in which you have to pay a fixed interest rate for a year's time and once the year ends, you get onto a variable rate mortgage. One year VRM plans are a combination of VRM and FRM. So, if you want to enjoy both types of mortgages by choosing this plan. However, when you pay a fixed interest rate for an entire year, you get used to managing your monthly payments. When you get onto a variable plan, you have to pay extremely high interest rates when the market rates are high. You also get to pay fairly low interest rates when the market rates go down.

10/1 VRM Plan

10/1 VRM is another mortgage plan suitable for those who want to enjoy perks of both types of mortgages; fixed and variable. In this mortgage plan, the borrower has to pay a fixed interest rate for ten years. This plan is usually offered for a 30 year plan. This means that you have to pay a fixed interest rate for 10 years and a variable interest rate for the remaining 20 years.

This mortgage plan is negotiable but requires you to pay a high interest rate for ten years. If this is not the type of mortgage that you are looking for and you want to enjoy lower interest rates, then you should opt for the one year VRM plan. If you do not agree with the interest rate offered by the lender, you can negotiate a lower rate for the FRM period.

Two-Step Mortgages

Another great VRM mortgage plan is the two-step mortgage. This type of mortgage plan allows borrowers to pay a fixed interest rate for 5 or 7 years and then continue with a variable interest rate. The interest rate for the fixed rate time period is determined before the deal is signed. So, you have a chance to negotiate a better rate with the lenders. However, keep in mind that the interest rates for the fixed rate period will be higher than the variable rate time period.

The two-year mortgage plan also has its perks. After your fixed rate mortgage period is over, you are free to choose whether you want to continue paying your pre-determined fixed interest rate for the rest of the mortgage repayment period or switch with a variable rate. This option is extremely beneficial for those borrowers who want to pick the most suitable option.

If you think that paying a fixed rate was more beneficial for you, then you can continue with the same plan. However, if you want to explore the second option and choose to pay a market-based interest rate, then you should have enough market knowledge. It is best to choose a variable rate plan if the market conditions point out towards lower interest rates. However, you should be aware that market rates fluctuate and where there are times that the interest rates fall, there are also times when the interest rates peak. So, beware and make the best decision for yourself.

Balloon Mortgages

The real estate business is growing in popularity due to the fact that it allows investors to earn maximum returns on their investments. That's one of the reasons that people from all walks of life are showing deep interest in this business and whether they are financially capable or not, they don't want to miss this great business opportunity. The people that do not have enough money to invest in real estate can opt for the options of loans and mortgages.

Balloon mortgage is another type of mortgage loan that allows borrowers to get rid of a greater percentage of their mortgage in the initial years of their repayment plan. However, the duration of this period is discussed between the lender and the borrower, and the lender usually makes the final decision. Some people might believe that this type of mortgage is risky and over burdening, but in reality, balloon mortgage allows borrowers to make most of their payments in the initial years and release most of the burden.

This repayment plan shed the burden that most borrowers feel towards the end of their repayment plan.

Applying for a Mortgage Plan

Getting a mortgage can be quite easy if you have a lot of money and a good credit history. However, when you don't have a lot of money, it can be challenging to convince a lender. The reason that lenders are really hard to convince is that many people who borrow money are unable to return it, especially the ones who do not have a job or enough bank balance. So, lenders have to contact them over and over again to get their money back. That's the reason lenders require to see that you are financially stable and have a secured job.

The Critical Lending Process

When you are applying for a mortgage plan, you need to meet certain criteria presented by the lender. These requirements often revolve around your financial conditions. Lenders have very strict rules and they scrutinize every borrower thoroughly to ensure that they are making a safe deal. Below is a list of requirements that many mortgage lenders require:

- Lenders will take a look at your past month's utility bills to see if you made your payments on time or not. They check bill payments to ensure that the person they are lending their money to is responsible enough to repay it on time.
- Lenders will ask for your total household income which will include bonds, increment, commissions, investments, and bonuses. They see this to ensure that you earn enough money and can handle a loan.
- Lenders will also take a look at your credit score to ensure that you are a responsible payer. They will check to see if you have made your loan and monthly payments on time. They will also look for any unresolved loans, which will give them a chance to say no to you. However, if your debt history is clear, there is a bright chance that you will be approved for the mortgage.
- Lenders will also ask for your credit history and if you have a bad credit history, they will not lend you any money. Bad credit history means that you have several faulty entries in your history. They also call the three credit unions to confirm about your credit history. If you have a bad credit history, lenders will not approve you because it simply means that you were unable to pay back your loan.
- Lenders will also ask for your major financial documents including pay slips, profit from investments, and your annual financial statements.

Lenders are extremely critical with their requirements because they cannot risk their money on someone who doesn't have the ability to pay their debts. If you meet their criteria and present yourself as a financially sound and stable person, then there is a high chance that you will get the loan that you want.

Preparing for the Application

Applying for a mortgage is a lengthy and stressful process. However, if you want the process to be less stressful, you need to make sure that you have your financial history in check. Before you head to the mortgage broker, make sure you have conducted a thorough evaluation of your financial statements. Be prepared because lenders will look at every tiny bit of detail to ensure that they are lending their money to the right person.

Make sure that you get a copy of your credit report from one of the three credit unions. This credit report holds a lot of importance in determining whether you will take the loan home or not. Getting a copy of your credit report is not the only job that you need to take care of. Make sure you conduct a thorough check that every information and entry in the report is legitimate. If you find any errors in the report, you can simply call the credit union and get it corrected. When you check your credit report, you are able to minimize the errors and maximize your chances of getting a loan.

Apart from credit report, make sure you collect all your important financial documents including your monthly earning, household expenses, earning from investments, and a list of your assets.

Documents Required by Lenders

In order to apply for a mortgage, you will need to collect necessary documents that your lender will ask you to bring along in the meeting. Below is a list of documents that your lender will require to review.

- Pay slips from the last three months.
- Copy of your utility bills from the last three months.
- Bank statements of your accounts from the past three to six months.
- Proof of your identification.
- Your passport.
- A document proving that you have filed your tax returns.
- Documents of income earned from other business or investment sources.
- Your driving license.
- A document including the benefits that you receive from your employer.
- A copy of your credit report from one of the three credit unions.
- A P60 form signed by your employer.
- Bank statements of your accounts and any other savings accounts.

Presenting the information isn't the only thing that you need to be careful about. Make sure that all the information mentioned in the documents is accurate. Any errors might create complications in your mortgage process. If there are any errors in the documents, you might not get approved for the loan. Moreover, if you try to trick the lenders by handing over false information to them, there is a high chance that you are going to get caught.

Lenders will double check the information that you provide to them. They will call your bank and the credit union to ensure that the entire information is accurate. If you get caught cheating on your lender, they will spread a bad word about you in the market, which will keep you from availing any type of loan opportunity.

Another thing that lenders often ask to disclose is the type of property that you are buying. They want to look at your investment to make sure that they are making a profitable deal. They also require looking at your property to come up with a suitable interest rate. If the property that you are buying is attractive and located in a place where the real estate market is booming, you might get approved for the mortgage.

Applying for a mortgage is not always complicated. It entirely depends on the lender that you opt for. Some lenders require very little information to approve a mortgage while others require detailed documents and information including original bank statements, utility bills, and financial documents. Some lenders also require you to give details on your overall monthly household expenditure and money spent on travelling and shopping. The reason that lenders ask for this information is that they want to see how much expenses are you capable of handling. This gives them a clearer idea of what to expect from you.

Once you have successfully submitted your mortgage application, you will get a call from your lender telling you whether the application is accepted or not. If your application is not accepted, you should try your luck elsewhere, but if you get the good news, you will be called for another meeting by the lender.

This meeting is usually for the purpose of negotiating a deal with mutual consent. It is better to take along all the necessary documents with you in the second meeting as well. This meeting's main purpose will be to set an interest fee, discuss on a plan, and assign a monthly payment. Lenders are often open to negotiations and discussions in their second meeting because they are also looking for a profitable deal.

Make sure you negotiate the interest rates and monthly payments. You will also get a chance to choose between fixed and variable mortgage. Now, this is the time you need to make a smart decision. If you have any knowledge about the real estate market, you will know what to pick. When choosing a monthly repayment plan, make sure you pick the one that is less stressful on you. You also need to consider the term of your repayment plan, as it determines the amount of interest you pay. The longer the term, the more money you will need to pay in the form of interest.

If you have been rejected for the mortgage, know that it is not the end of the world. You can ask the lender for another meeting so that you can negotiate with them. When you finally meet with the lender, you ask them to pinpoint the things that caused them to disapprove of the mortgage. By looking at these things, you can make out whether the issues were justified or not. If errors were due to negligence from any agency or financial institution, then you can ask for a second chance.

Hiring an Accountant

Accountants are highly skilled individuals who have experience with financial studies. When you are having troubles in getting a loan, your accountant can help you get through the process with ease. When you are denied for a mortgage, an accountant will help devise a financial plan for you to present it to the lender. This financial plan will help you design a payment schedule to help the lender have faith in you and your capability to pay back the loan.

When the accountant has designed a repayment plan for you, you can present it to the lender to make them believe that you can pay it back. Although it happens very rarely, if you make a good argument, there are high chances that your application will be accepted. An accountant can also help design a financial plan for you when you have received the mortgage. They will help design a repayment and savings plan, so that you can get rid of your mortgage as soon as possible.

Managing Mortgage Payments Responsibly

Once you have received the mortgage, it is time to focus on a repayment plan. The biggest challenge for borrowers comes up after they have received the mortgage. When borrowers fail to repay their debts and secure their investment, lenders have no option but to take their assets from them. This happens because borrowers fail to make regular monthly payments and meet mortgage criteria.

Poor debt management is caused when borrowers fail to manage their money. In order to manage your debts in a better way, you need to calculate your overall monthly income, minus the household expenses. The amount that will be left will go to your savings account, out of which you will take out your debt payments. Calculating your expenses and savings is the best way to ensure that you pay your debts responsibly.

A great motivation to make regular debt repayments is to think about the assets that the mortgage is secured by. Let's say you have secured your loan with your home. So, if you are unable to pay back your loan, your home will be taken by lenders and put up on foreclosure sale. This will make you lose your most prized asset, which is enough to stay motivated to pay your debts on time.

Monthly Cash flow

When you have taken a home loan, it is important that you work on creating a repayment plan. The most important thing to keep in mind when designing a debt management plan is to keep a track of your monthly cash flow. Your monthly cash flow is your income that you use to pay utility bills and handle other household expenses.

When you borrow money to buy a property, you are aware that it is a huge amount of money that you now owe to someone. Therefore, it is important to realize that your first priority should be to pay back that loan quickly. Therefore, you need to be frugal with your expenses. Try not to waste money on things that you do not need. This way you will be able to save enough to repay your loan on a monthly basis.

However, it is best to make greater payments so that you can get rid of your loan in fewer years. This is great for saving money on hefty interest rates that many lenders apply on home mortgages. Paying your mortgage before the decided time period will be more beneficial for borrowers who have opted for fixed rate mortgages. Because fixed rate mortgages usually have a higher interest rate, borrowers can save a lot of money by repaying the loan before the designated time.

Designate Extra Profit towards Debt Repayment

Borrowing money to invest in real estate means that you are dealing with thousands of dollars. Spending on the property, sometimes the loan amount reaches up to millions of dollars. This means that you have to be very smart in handling your finances. Apart from your fixed income, you need to find other ways to collect money for loan repayment.

A good way to earn extra money is to make use of your real estate investment. You can rent your property to earn money off of it and designate that profit to a separate savings account meant for debt payments only.

Do not extend the Debt Repayment Plan

One cannot stress less on the fact that debt can become quite a burden for a borrower, especially when it is a home mortgage. In order to feel relaxed and stress-free, you should design such a repayment plan that allows you to get rid of your loan before the actual time period.

Another reason for paying your debt quickly is to earn maximum profit out of your investment. Because you are looking to make your monthly debt repayments, you will not be able to truly enjoy the profit coming to you in the form of rent. However, when you don't have debt to repay, you can easily save all the money you receive from rent. In order to enjoy a great ROI, you need to devise a strategy to save as much money as possible and return the loan in less time.

Many real estate investors make a mistake of quitting their job once they start to earn sound profit from their investments. Although it might seem like you are all set to earn massive in the real estate business, there is still a lot to learn. Therefore, even if you start to earn a good return on your first few investments, do not make the mistake of quitting your job. The money that you earn from your job is a fixed monthly cash flow. However, the profit coming from your investments is not fixed. Sometimes you might earn more and some days you'll earn less.

Once you have enough experience dealing with real estate investments, you can think about quitting your job. But before that point, do not make this mistake, especially when you are under debt.

Chapter 7: Buying Properties On Lease

If you are attracted to the real estate business but do not have enough money to buy a property upfront, then you might want to consider the option of leasing. Leasing is another attractive option for people who cannot afford to buy properties. This option is also suitable for those who do not want to opt for home mortgages.

Leasing homes is very similar to renting one because you have to pay a monthly amount to the owner of the property. Let's say you are interested in buying a home which costs $100, 000, but you do not have enough cash. Because you don't want to lose the property, you reach out to the owner and ask for leasing the home. The owner agrees to it and asks you to pay $2000/month for fifty months to cover the entire cost of the home. This is what leasing is all about.

However, leasing option is very hard to get as many owners aren't ready to take this risk with their properties. When you lease a property, you actually own the property until you cover its entire value. It's common for people to opt for the option of leasing because not everyone is able to pay a huge cost upfront. Let's take a look into the leasing option in detail.

All about Leasing a Property

The option of leasing is suitable for almost anyone. Whether you were denied for mortgage or your credit score wasn't good enough, you don't have to worry as you can lease a property that you are interested in. Because getting a loan or a mortgage is a tough task, it is usual for people to opt for the option of leasing. Let's find out more about leasing, its advantages, and disadvantages as well.

Buy homes on lease

So, you have sighted a property that you are interested in buying, but when you check your bank accounts, you do not have enough to pay the property's price. You meet with a lender to ask for a loan, but due to certain circumstances, the lender rejects you. You are disappointed and you opt for a mortgage plan but due to your low credit score, you once again face rejection.

Instead of feeling low and disappointed, you have a chance to opt for the option of lease to invest in your dream property. The option of lease is easier than loan or mortgage. However, when you lease a property, you are required to pay 3%-5% of the property's price upfront. Now, this can be a problem for those who cannot afford this either.

The down payment of the property can keep you from purchasing the property of your dreams. Therefore, if you think that you would want to invest in real estate, start saving now. Save enough money that you can make the down payment and enjoy the perks of leasing.

Protection against the Fluctuating Market

When buyers want to opt for a loan, they usually pick the option of lease financing because it offers the highest perks. Lease financing is a secure option that will protect you from the fluctuating market. This means that when the market rates go down, you have the option to opt-out of the deal. Similarly, when the market goes up, you can continue with the lease and increase the equity on the home.

Lower Monthly Payments

When you opt for the option of mortgage, you will be paying a higher monthly fee, which is inflicted with interest. This is not the case with lease financing as the monthly fee is based on the rates that you and the owners agreed upon. So, even when the market rates go up, you pay a lower rate. Mortgages on the other hand fluctuate with the market. Even when you opt for a variable rate mortgage, you have to pay a higher interest rate than lease financing.

No more pressure from the bank

Another great perk of lease financing is that it has nothing to do with the bank. The most stressful thing about mortgages and loans is that you have to deal with the bank if you are unable to make your payments. Lenders also require that the loan be secured by an asset, which is usually in the form of a car or the home itself. This means that even if you are unable to make your payments, you will not lose your assets. However, not making monthly payments in a lease agreement means that you will no longer be able to own the home.

How do you qualify for Lease Financing?

If you are interested in the lease financing option, you should be aware that there are certain criteria that you need to fulfill to get approved for this option. Let's take a look below:

Credit Report

When you opt for lease financing, the owner of the home will ask to see your credit report. Owners review the credit report because it gives them a clear idea of what the applicant is capable of and their financial standing. Your credit report will also be a proof of your responsible behavior. If there are lots of debts in your report, there is a high chance that you might get rejected for the lease.

Whether you are going for the option of loan, mortgage, or lease, your credit report will play a prominent role in it. By looking at the credit report, owner of the home will be able to make a decision. If your report proves that you are a responsible payer, you are most likely to get approved.

Income

If you do not have a flowing income, no one will ever agree to sign a lease option with you. In order to buy a home on lease, you need to have a flowing income. Although lease financing is not as complicated and strict as mortgage and loan financing, it still requires the applicants to have a source of income. Owners do not want to seal a risky deal.

That's the reason it is important for every applicant to show a proof of their source of income.

Sealing the Lease Deal

When it comes to lease financing, you need to make sure that you will buy the property at the end of the contract. Moreover, you have to ensure that you are capable of paying the monthly fees to secure the home or else you will lose money. So, after you have reviewed your options, it is time to make the decision.

When it is time to make a decision, it is important to consider your financial conditions and affordability factor. If you have enough money to afford a mortgage, then do not opt for lease financing. However, if you cannot afford a mortgage, then you have no option but to go for lease. When you lease a property, you are actually renting it until you cover its entire cost.

It is also important to keep an eye on the property, especially if you are not living in it. This means you need to conduct regular inspections to ensure that the property is in perfect shape. Another thing to keep in mind when opting for lease financing is that you should be able to afford taxes, maintenance costs, and utility bills of the leased property.

The monthly payments in the lease financing option are predetermined, which means that they are set at the time of contract finalization. So, whether the market goes up or down, you will be paying a fixed rate. This can sometimes be bad for you when the market is down, because you still have to pay a fixed monthly fee without any discount.

Real estate investments are not a piece of cake. Buying a property means that you have to prepare yourself to spend, a lot for that matter. Therefore, if you want to save a little money, try your luck in negotiating the rates with the seller. You can also negotiate on down payment and monthly fee. If you think you cannot afford a higher monthly fee, ask the seller to lower it down. Your negotiations will help you get a good deal.

If you think that this option is for you, go for it.

Things to watch out for

Before you make a decision, you need to make sure you consider a few factors. Because you are relying on the property's owner for a favor, you need to be very careful. Sometimes lease financing may seem like the best option, but in order to make the most of it, you need to weigh every factor. Below are some factors that you need to consider before going for the lease option.

Do you have enough money?

Before you opt for lease financing, ask yourself whether you can afford the down payment or not. If you do not have enough money, you will not be able to pay the property's 3%-5% value upfront to the owner. Go for this option only if you can afford the down payment or else opt for a mortgage. You need to make sure that you are able to manage your finances in such a way that you make regular monthly payments or else you might even lose money.

Do not walk out of the deal

It is true that lease financing is an attractive option, but if you abandon the deal in the middle of the contract, you will incur a huge loss. The money that you pay in the form of monthly fee will not be returned to you even if you are no longer willing to buy the home. This means that you will not get your money back. So, when you are getting into a deal, make sure you will stick to it for the entire course of the contract.

Does the property require extensive maintenance?

Before you sign the lease contract, make sure you conduct property inspection. Examining the property will help you find out flaws in it. If you come across several things that need improvement, then ask the seller to either lower the rates or make the necessary repairs. Properties that require extensive maintenance have a greater chance to be sold at lower rates. This point will help you during negotiations.

Lease financing is undoubtedly a golden chance for people to buy their desired properties. However, if you don't want things to turn against you, evaluate your financial standing and make sure you pay your monthly fee. Once the lease period is over, you can relax and enjoy owning a new property that you can use to earn great profits.

Chapter 8: Why Investing In Foreclosed Properties Is A Good Option

Foreclosure Homes

When looking to buy properties at cheaper rates, one cannot overlook the option of foreclosures. Foreclosure homes or properties are the ones that are sold by lenders. Lenders are looking to sell the property to cover their costs that the homeowner was unable to pay in the form of a loan. Therefore, these properties are usually sold at an auction and are priced less than new properties.

Foreclosure homes are perfect for investment, especially for people who do not have a great bank balance. If you are looking to invest in real estate with little money, there is nothing better than buying a property in a pre-foreclosure sale. The reason that these homes are sold at cheaper rates is that lenders are desperate to gain back their money, and to do so they have to sell the borrowers' assets. Buying homes in foreclosure sale definitely seems like an appealing offer. Let's take a look at how it works in detail.

Buying Homes in Pre-Foreclosure Sale

When you are planning to buy a home in a pre-foreclosure sale, it is better to do your homework and learn how it works before taking part in it. Moreover, you cannot just blindly make a deal on a foreclosure home without investigating and evaluating the property carefully. Many times foreclosure homes end up making buyers lose money. Because these are not like the typical property auctions, there is a high chance that these properties are damaged or not worth it.

In order to avoid losing thousands of dollars, you need to earn about the process of buying a property in a pre-foreclosure sale. Let's take a look at how the process works.

Look for a Foreclosure Property

If you are interested in buying a foreclosed property, you should find it first. Finding a property listed for a pre-foreclosure sale is a difficult task. However, the best place to find such a sale or auction is to look in your local newspaper. Make sure you check the newspaper on a daily basis for any pre-foreclosure auction announcements because that's your best bet at finding one.

Pay a Visit to the Property

Once you have found a property on foreclosure auction, it is time to visit it. Foreclosure properties are risky and that's the reason you need to take out time to examine them. By visiting the property, you will also be able to get a good idea of its location. The ROI on your real estate investment depends on the location of the property, if the property is located in an attractive neighborhood; there is a high chance that you will attract more buyers, renters, and get greater profit. A good way to get to know about the neighborhood is to talk to others living in it.

It is not always easy to get a good deal on a foreclosed property

Although there is information available about buying foreclosed properties in an auction, there is still a very slight chance that you will seal a profitable deal. The reason that many realtors and market experts suggest not to invest in foreclosed properties is that they are very risky, especially for the people who are new in the real estate business.

However, if you want to buy a foreclosed home at a good deal minus the risk, you should contact a realtor who has experience picking the most attractive properties. An experienced realtor will offer properties that are thoroughly examined. So, there are less chances of buying a damaged property.

Chapter 9: Investing To Sell

When it comes to earning an income out of your real estate investment, you will come across two options; invest to sell or invest to rent. As a real estate investor, you should always be in search of a profitable opportunity to make the most of your investment. However, you need to make this important decision very smartly.

The option of selling a property has its own share of advantages and disadvantages. However, if you have proper market knowledge, you will be able to make the best decision. Flipping properties is something that people with experience in real estate do.

Examine Market Conditions

The most important thing that you need to keep in mind when planning to sell properties is that you have to keep an eye on the market. If the market rates are on the lower side, it is best to avoid selling a property because you will not make any profit. However, if the market is going well and the properties are becoming more valuable, only then you think about selling yours.

Re-consider Your Decision

It is not always about selling your property at a good rate. Sometimes you just have to reconsider your decision to think about long-term benefits. When the market is going up, you can think of putting the property up for rent as it will give you a flowing monthly income. There are several factors that you need to keep in mind when making a decision for your property, because it is all about money and earning profits, keep in mind that the option of renting allows you to earn better profits in the long run, especially when the market is going up.

Make a Wise Decision

In the end, it is all about your market knowledge and experience in real estate properties. If you believe that the value of your property will never be as high as it is at a particular time, then you can think about selling it. However, if you believe that the value of your property will continue to increase, you can hold onto your property and think about other options such as putting it up for rent.

Your Property is a Valuable Asset

The people who are new to the real estate business or have invested in a property for the first time need to be aware of the fact that the property they have is a valuable asset. If you do not plan to invest in more homes, it is good to keep the property to yourself.

However, it is true that most people who invest in real estate for the first time want to continue investing in more due to the high margin of profits. So, if that's the case with you too, you can sell the property only when the market is going up.

Do Your Research About the Location of the Property

Selling a property is a crucial decision. There are many factors that play their role in determining whether the property should be sold or kept. A great way to know about the value of your property is to research about the location. Certain locations are more valuable than others. Their value is often determined by the places near the location, amenities, view, recreation, and much more. So, before selling your property, take a look at the location and research about it.

If the neighborhood in which the property is located is tagged as valuable and the rates are constantly going up, then it is best to keep the property. The best thing about continually increasing value is that even when the market goes down, you do not lose money. Therefore, it is important to buy properties in locations that are valuable or that have a potential to improve.

Investing To Rent-Out

When you invest in real estate properties, there are normally two options that you can opt for; rent-out or sell. Because selling investment properties is already covered above, let's talk about renting-out a property.

Different investors think differently, but when it comes to profit, they want to make sure that they are earning the most. Selling an investment property means that you will no longer be the owner. However, renting out a property means that you not only have a valuable asset in hand, you are also earning additional monthly income out of it.

Renting out is sometimes the most appealing option for investors because they want to earn flowing monthly income without any worries. They also have both the options available to them; earn rent or sell it. Let's find out whether renting is a good option or not.

Low Market Rates

Renting out your property means that you are still the owner. Many investors opt for this option when they are unable to sell their properties or are not willing to sell them at a lower rate. If the market is going down and the value of your property has decreased, it is best to rent the property out. By renting it out, you will at least earn money from it, which is better than selling it at a lower rate.

Rental Income

The biggest perk of renting an income property is that you get to enjoy monthly income. Everyone who is part of the real estate business is looking to earn more money in one way or another. The income that you earn from your rental property can be utilized in a number of ways. You can make use of this income to pay your mortgage, taxes, and much more. You can also use it to manage the property.

Renting Out Multiple Properties

You reap the benefits of rental income the most when you own multiple properties because you get to earn monthly income from several sources. The option of putting your property on rent is extremely beneficial in any case. Even if you do not have multiple homes, you can choose this option to earn money.

Cost of Property Management

If you are choosing the option of renting out your property, you would need to look into the additional costs that come with it. This option might attract many first time investors, but you should be aware that having tenants is a huge responsibility. Because the property belongs to you, you have to manage it, pay mortgages, and file taxes. These costs can add up to become a lot. Therefore, before making your final decision, take your time to calculate the amount of money that you will earn as compared to the money that you will be spending.

Property management is essential if you have rented out your property, especially if you have multiple properties and tenants. It helps manage everything including rent collection, repairs, and tenant problems. Although you can handle these chores on your own, if you have multiple tenants, it is better to hire a property manager to do the tasks. However, you should be aware that property managers charge fee, which means that you will need to pay them from your pocket. If you are ready to pay the fee, then you can opt for this option.

Whether you are investing to sell or investing to rent-out, it is important to weigh every factor before making a decision. Sometimes it is more profitable to sell a home than rent it and vice versa.

Chapter 10: The Benefits Of Buying Investment Properties

The real estate market has become an attraction for people who want to invest and earn profits. Because there is a huge profit margin in investment properties, almost everyone is interested in pursuing it as a business career. The rich and the middle-class are all interested in buying properties then either selling them or putting them up for rent.

The only reason behind this increasing trend is that you can earn huge returns on your investments. However, when you are new to the real estate business, you have to be careful in picking the most attractive properties for investment. If you get everything right, you can earn massive. Let's take a look at the benefits of buying investment properties. These benefits will convince you to invest in real estate today.

Valuable Asset

The biggest perk of investing in real estate is that you get hold of a valuable asset. When you buy a property, you have the option to either keep it for yourself or sell it to earn greater returns. If you are new to the business, you will most likely be looking to sell or rent the property to earn profits. However, if you have multiple properties at hand, you would want to secure one for yourself.

Because properties are valuable, they are counted as part of your wealth. This is a great way to protect yourself from financial loss in the future. If you secure a property for yourself, you can make use of it when you need money by selling or renting it out. You can also earn a flowing income from your property.

You Own the Property

Investing to buy a property means that it will be under your name and you will be its owner. Being the owner of a property is a huge deal as it is a valuable asset that can give you great returns.

Diversification of your Portfolio

When you invest in real estate properties, you are actually diversifying your asset portfolio. Real estate belongs to a distinct asset class, which helps add variety to your portfolio. Furthermore, your investment properties can be used as sources of income; they become the most valuable asset class.

You can Earn Flowing Income by Renting the Property

Once you have bought a property, you know you are the boss and you can use it anyway. You can either run your office in it or you can rent it out. However, renting is the most attractive option for real estate investors, as it helps them earn a flowing income on a monthly basis.

You can Increase its Value

The properties that you invest in are your tangible assets, which means that you can make physical changes to it. So, if you make changes to the property like improving a certain area of the property, repairing different systems, installing high-tech appliances, etc, you can increase its price. This way you can earn a lot more than you initially invested in the property. These improvements also prove beneficial in increasing the rent on the house.

You can get rid of Taxes on your Income Property

Although the income earned from rental properties is taxable, as a landlord, you can still enjoy lots of deductions. Below is a list of tax deductions that you can enjoy on your investment properties.

- The interest that you pay on your mortgage loan for the maintenance and repair of your rental property can be deducted.
- If you are purchasing goods for the improvement of your rental property through your credit card, then the interest on the payment can be deducted.
- If you are making any necessary repairs to your rental property, then the amount of money that you spend will be tax deductible. However, the repairs should be basic and reasonable.
- If the value of your property depreciates over the years, then you can receive deductions on tax.
- If you are travelling anywhere for the purpose of your rental property, then it will come under deductible income. This also includes gas expenses.
- If you are travelling long distances for any rental activity, then you can deduct the expenses of airfare, meals, hotel bills, and much more.
- If you have a personal office for managing your rental activities, then you can get deductions on its expenses.

Chapter 11: Real Estate Investor Tax Implications

The real estate market has become a magnet for investors looking to earn great returns. However, what many first time investors don't understand is that their investments will be taxed. Because you are investing to earn profits, it is understood that you will have to pay taxes. Therefore, you need to be prepared to pay taxes before you enter into the real estate business.

Taxes can be hard to manage, but if you understand how they work, you can keep your business running without any glitches. As real estate investors, you need to understand that any income that you earn should be reported to the IRS. Let's dig deeper into tax implications for real estate investors.

Rental Income Tax

Any type of income that you earn from the property that you own is taxable. This also includes the income that you earn from rent. Even if a tenant pays you a certain amount of money for maintenance and repairs, this income should also be reported to the IRS. You should also report any money that you save from the maintenance cost given to you by the tenants.

If you sell your property, you have to report the income earned because it is also taxable. You have to notify the IRS of any rental income that you earn from your properties. The good news is that you can get deductions on certain expenses related to your rental properties. Apart from your immediate rental income, you need to report other types of income related to your property as well. Take a look below.

Alex Lee

Advance Rent

The monthly rental income is not the only income that you report to the IRS. The advance rent that you take from tenants is also taxable, which means that you need to mention it too. Let's say the monthly rent that you earn from a property is $5000 and you ask for an additional $5000 as an advance rent for the last year of the lease. This means that you have to mention $10, 000 as your rental income for that year.

Security Deposit

Security deposits are usually meant to be returned to the tenants at the end of the lease. However, if your tenant is unable to make complete payments, you get to keep the security deposit, which means that you have to report it to the IRS in the same year. Once the security deposit turns into an income, it becomes taxable. However, if you are return it back to the tenants, you do not have to count it under your income.

Lease Cancellation Payment

Sometimes when a tenant wants to cancel the lease, they pay you a certain amount of money. This money is termed as rental income, which means that it will be taxed. This payment that you receive should be added to your income and listed in the tax application.

Expenses Paid by Tenants

Although tenants aren't supposed to pay extra expenses for the property, but if they are, then you need to include them in your earned income. If your tenant has paid the utility bills, the amount of money that they pay will be deducted from the monthly rent that they pay. The amount that is deducted from their rent should also be reported as it is taxable.

Similarly, if you asked your tenants to pay for improvements and maintenance, this amount will also be termed as income and will be taxed.

Additional Services

If your tenant tells you that they can take care of the improvement in the home, and in turn ask you to cancel out the rent for two months, then you will have to report the rent of two months to the IRS. Because maintenance and improvement is the landlord's job, and if the tenant is paying for it, you have to count the revoked rent as earned income.

Capital Gains

When you own an asset that you sell out for a price higher than the price you bought it for, it counts as capital gains and is also a taxable income. However, capital gains do not count when you still own the asset. Because the real estate business depends upon the profit earned from selling properties at a higher rate, the income earned out of your investments is counted as capital gains tax.

Land Tax

Land tax is simply the tax on the value of a property. This means that whenever you make a real estate investment, you have to pay a certain amount of money as tax.

When you are in the real estate business or planning to enter it, you need to understand the different taxes involved in it. Every time you make an investment for the sake of earning profits, you have to pay back to the government. However, when it comes to deductions, there is a lot that you can get subtracted. Continue reading onto the next chapter where you will find the different types of tax deductions that you can claim on your properties.

Chapter 12: Tax Deductions For Landlords On Rental Properties

Most part of your rental income is taxable, but there are several instances in which you can save some money through deductibles. When you have a clear knowledge about tax deductibles, you are able to make the most of them to save a great part of your rental income from tax.

Insurance Premiums

If you are paying insurance for different rental activities like fire protection, flood insurance, and landlord liability insurance, then you can get their premiums deducted. If you have a well-settled rental or real estate business, and you have hired employees, then you can deduct workers compensation and health insurance.

Professional Services

The real estate investors that have a big rental or property business often need the help of realtors, accountants, and property managers. So, if you are hiring these professionals for work related to your rental business, you can get them deducted.

Casualty Losses

If your rental property has been damaged by a natural calamity or theft, you can get a part of those expenses deducted from your taxes. However, if you already got it covered by insurance, you have to look into the amount that you can get deducted. Sometimes the entire cost of damage is tax deductible.

Independent Contractors

Let's say you have to get something fixed at your rental property and you hire an independent contractor. So, the fee that you pay the contractor will be counted as deductible. Similarly, when you hire employees to perform services for your rental activity, you can get their pay deducted from your rental income tax too.

Office Space

A real estate investor who is starting their own rental business often requires an office space to conduct business operations from. The cost of office space that you purchase to conduct your rental business operations can be deducted. This also includes any other services that you use like telephone and internet. You can also get the furnishing costs deducted from your annual taxes.

Travelling Costs

When you own a rental business, you have to travel from place to place to get things done. Whenever you have to travel for the sake of your rental business, you can deduct the cost spent in your tax returns. If you travel by car, you can get the cost of gasoline deducted. However, you have to make use of the standard mileage rate. Make sure to take a look at the IRS website to find out about the current rates.

In case your car requires repair while you are traveling for performing any rental business activity, you can get that cost deducted too.

Sometimes you have properties in different locations. So, if you have to travel long distances to conduct business operations, you can deduct that cost too. This deduction includes airfare, hotel bills, meals, and other expenses. However, when it comes to long distance travelling, the IRS looks closely into the details and then approves deductions. If you don't want to end up losing money and missing out on a good tax deduction opportunity, make sure you check the IRS website to follow the rules.

Interest

One of the greatest tax deduction opportunities for landlords lies in interest payments. If you are paying interest on a mortgage plan or loan, you can get it deducted. Even when you are purchasing goods or spending money on a service related to your rental property, you can get the interest on your credit card deducted.

When you borrow a loan or are part of a mortgage plan, you have to pay a lot of money in interest. The interest rate changes depending on the marketed conditions. There are times when the interest rates in the market are going down, and there are times when they are going up. These increased interest rates can increase your monthly mortgage repayment greatly, especially if you have a variable rate mortgage. However, when you know that you can get the interest amount deducted, you can save a lot of money.

Repairs

Landlords are responsible for fixing problems in their properties. That's the reason they get regular calls from the renters for getting something repaired or remodeled. The cost of repairs and improvements can increase dramatically, causing the landlords to lose a lot of money.

However, there is good news for landlords as they can subtract the ordinary repairs and improvements they make to their rental properties including a new paintjob, repairing leaky gutters, replacing faucets, and much more. This money spent on repairs and improvements can be deducted from the year that they were incurred.

Phone Bills

As a landlord you have to stay in touch with the property managers, service guys, and the renters. This means that you have to make use of your phone to make important calls. When you call several times a day, it can cost you a lot of money. The good news is that landlords can deduct the tax on their phone bills, given that the calls they make are for their rental business purpose.

These amazing tax deductions on your rental properties can prove to be extremely beneficial. These deductions not only help save money, but exert a lower financial pressure on investors.

Chapter 13: Different Ways You Can Earn ROI On Your Investment Property

Anyone who is looking to enter into the real estate business wants to earn great returns. It is obvious that when someone is investing a certain amount of money, they are taking a risk because return is not guaranteed. Even though the investments we make are packed with risks, we still aim for them to turn into lucrative financial decisions.

The biggest opportunity for earning great returns is the real estate business. Everyone that has enough money is ready to invest their money into a property, but when it comes to calculating the ROI, no one really understands the mathematical calculations. There is a simple formula to calculate the ROI i.e. **Return ÷ Total Amount Paid Out of Pocket = ROI**

Once you divide the return you earn by selling your investment property with the amount of money that you initially invested in it, you will get result in points. When you divide the result by 100, you get a percentage, which is the ROI you earned.

Calculating the ROI on the properties that you sell is easy, but calculating the ROI on the properties that you put up for rent is a little tricky as you are not getting a return in a defined form. Let's take a deeper look at the concept of ROI, as it is the most important thing that every real estate investor is worried about.

Long-Term Rental Properties

When you invest in real estate for the sake of earning a massive ROI, you need to consider putting your properties up for rent. Rental income is considered the perkiest in the real estate business. However, you need to make sure that you have several properties on rent for a long period of time. Renting out a property for a few months or even a year will not help you earn massive returns. The rental properties that are being rented out for several years are the most lucrative ones.

Even when you plan to put your properties on rent for a long period of time, there are certain factors that determine whether you will be earning a higher return or not. Let's find out the different ways you can accelerate returns on your long-term rental property investments.

Buy Properties at below Market Rates

Buying properties and then putting them up for rent is not the only thing that you should be focusing on. The main purpose of your investment is to improve the cash flow on your rental properties. But how would you be able to improve the cash flow if recovering the investment amount is taking several years? This means that if you want to earn a great ROI on your rental properties, you need to purchase properties at below market value. Let's help you understand it in a better way.

Let's say you purchase a property for $150, 000 and you put it up for rent. The monthly rent that you collect is $2000(Net). Now, when you divide the investment amount by the monthly rent, you will get 75, which is the number of months it will take for you to recover the entire investment cost.

The length of time to recoup your initial investment may even be shorter as the monthly rental goes up periodically.

However, if you bought a property at a lower rate, you will easily be able to recover the investments amount, and will get to enjoy returns as well.

That's the reason it is better to buy a property at a lower rate, which will make it easier for you to not only recover the cost but also earn returns in a short period of time.

Make Improvements

Buying a home at lower rate means that it will not be as attractive as the other higher priced homes in the neighborhood. When a property is sold at a lower cost, it often means that it has a lot of repairs and improvement issues. This means that you have to be really careful when looking for properties to purchase. If you are buying from a reputable investor, you will get hold of a good property. In case the property is greatly damaged, do not opt for it. However, if the improvements and repairs are minor, do not miss out on a cheap deal. By spending extra money out of your pocket to get the home fixed, you will be able to attract several tenants.

A well maintained home is the one that gets rented out for a good price. This will allow you to earn a good monthly rent, which will make it easy for you to get great ROI within a short period of time. The ROI that you earn from long-term rental properties depends on the number of properties that you have rented out. The more properties you put up on rent, the greater are your chances to earn huge returns.

Profits on Increased Property Value

When people invest in real estate, they are mostly looking to sell the property as soon as the prices go up. This means that high returns can be earned from real estate investments when you sell the property at a rate higher than the rate that you bought it for. Flipping homes is the most common practice in the real estate business.

However, the property value doesn't increase without any reason. The value increases when you fix the home or make big improvements. This is similar to buying cheap homes and then fixing them to increase their value. Although you are spending thousands of dollars on repairs and improvements, you still get to increase the price of your property greatly.

The money you put in improvements entirely depends on your experience. If you know contractors that work at cheap rates, you will be able to enjoy maximum profits. Similarly, when you opt for expensive contractors, you end up losing money.

Property Improvements and Renovations

The real estate business is all about making smart financial decisions. So, if you are looking to sell your properties at a much higher rate to earn huge ROI, you need invest your time, money, and efforts into improving the look of the home. By making simple improvements and renovations, you can increase a property's value greatly. However, if you do not have experience performing repairs and improvements, stay away from it. Many people make this mistake of performing the improvements on their own, which not only takes up a lot of their time; it also becomes extremely expensive and tiring. Therefore, get in touch with a professional contractor and negotiate the rates with them. These contractors will help reduce stress, and save your precious time and money.

Remodeling a room or the kitchen will also help increase its value in the market, allowing you to sell at a higher rate. When picking the area to renovate, make sure you consider the rooms that home owners are most likely to focus on. Nowadays, the focal point of every home is its kitchen. The kitchen not only acts as a place for cooking purposes, but it has become more of a sitting area. By remodeling a kitchen, you can attract several potential buyers to your property.

It is important to know that whether you are looking to sell the property or put it up for rent, remodeling or improvements can make a huge difference on its price. So, if you want to earn huge returns on your investment, try opting for this option.

Paying Off the Mortgage Early

When you buy properties on mortgage, you do not realize that you have signed a contract to pay a lot of money every month for several years. Now that you realize that your mortgage is a huge responsibility and a great financial burden, you begin to feel stressed. Well, stress is not the only concerning factor about mortgage payments.

We live in a really unpredictable economy that in the past has faced inflation twice. This means that you don't have a solid job security, and God forbid if the economy goes down, you will be unable to make these payments on a regular basis. When you consider factors like these, you realize that mortgage has become more of a problem for you than an opportunity. That's the reason many professional advisors suggest that we make our mortgage payments before the actual time period.

When you repay the entire mortgage amount, you are able to earn returns on your investment properties. Let's say you bought a property on mortgage and put it up for rent. Because you have to make monthly repayments, you are unable to enjoy the rent that you get every month. Furthermore, this ongoing mortgage payment can keep you from enjoying great returns. So, it is better to pre-pay your mortgage than to complete its time-period.

Another great reason to pre-pay your mortgage is that the value of money is always fluctuating, and it usually depreciates. So, the return that you earn out of your investment property twenty years later might not be as valuable as the returns that you earn today. So, if you are looking to maximize the ROI on your real estate properties, try getting rid of your mortgage before the designated time.

Making Money through Wholesale Properties

Wholesaling properties is another great option for investors to earn great returns on their real estate investments. Wholesaling in real estate stands for the properties that you buy under a contract without taking ownership. This means that you don't have to repair the properties. All you need to do is sell the contract to another investor. This option allows investors to earn lots of money without any risk.

The greatest thing about these properties is that they are sold by owners who are in a rush to sell their homes. There are many people who are either too caught up to look for realtors to list their property in the market or they are residing in another place. This means that in order to find wholesale contracts, you need to look for properties off the market. The sellers of such properties often have one purpose in mind; to sell the property as soon as possible without digging too deep into the rates.

Make sure that you look into your state laws before opting for this option, as many states haven't legalized wholesale property investments.

Invest in Properties in Other Locations

Sometimes investing in real estate becomes troubling when you are unable to find interesting properties in the area you live in. When people don't find suitable properties in their area, they often give-up on the idea of investing in real estate. However, the real estate business has no boundaries, which means that you are free to choose properties in different locations (of course in the same city or country).

If the properties in a certain neighborhood are sold at higher rates, look for a cheaper neighborhood where you can see potential. Buying properties at a higher rate is not a good idea, especially if you are looking to earn a cash flow. So, head to another neighborhood or city if you are having trouble finding cheap properties near you. Investing in properties that are present in different locations is also a good way to diversify your real estate investment portfolio. However, along with advantages come disadvantages. Buying properties in different locations will require you to spend more money on travelling. Furthermore, when you invest in a new location, you need to get to know it. This means that you will need to get in touch with a local realtor to find out about the market conditions. This will also require a lot of time, money, and efforts from your side. If done correctly, this can prove to be extremely beneficial, helping you earn huge returns.

Let's take a look at some tips that will help you pick the best properties in different locations for greater returns.

➢ *Find a Suitable Market*

You cannot just pick a location and buy properties. In order to make a financially sound decision, you need to dig deep into the details. This means that you will need to pick a location after conducting extensive research. If you have a particular area or neighborhood in mind, try to investigate about it. Talk to the people living in that community and the realtors. This will help give you a good idea about the area's real estate market and its conditions.

Spend a solid amount of time researching about the area that you are interested in. Once you get to know that the location is good for real estate investments, you can move onto the next step.

➢ *Get in Touch with a Good Realtor*

When you are investing in long-distance properties, you need to take help from a realtor. Realtors are of great help to the investors. Because they have a complete know-how of the market, they can help investors make sound decisions. When it comes to long-distance investments, there is nothing more important than getting in touch with an experienced realtor.

Because you are unaware of the new location, a realtor will help find great property deals for you. They will also prove to be beneficial in picking the right properties by getting them inspected for you. Realtors can also save you from making bad investment decisions, as they have greater knowledge about the market that they are a part of.

➢ *Look for a Property Manager*

The most essential aspect of long-distance real estate investment is to hire a property manager. Property managers take care of everything. From maintaining the property to collecting rents, they do it all. The work that they do helps long-distance investors enjoy peace of mind, and at the same time keeping their properties in perfect shape. Property managers play an important role in rental properties, as they are responsible for collecting rents and hearing out the problems of the tenants. They are also a way of communication between the landlord and the tenants. This means that when you are investing in rental properties outside your area, you must hire a property manager.

Due to their connections in the market, they are also great for getting most of your job done including hiring contractors for maintaining the property. They can help save lots of money by hiring cheap contractors. They will also collect rent from the tenants, without causing any hassle. Furthermore, if the tenants have any complaints or queries, they can contact the property manager, who is available 24/7.

➢ *Find a Suitable Contractor*

Although most property managers are responsible for hiring contractors, if your property manager doesn't offer this service, you have to find someone on your own. Finding a property manager is a tough job because they are expensive and most of them are not really trustworthy. When it comes to finding a contractor in another location, it becomes tougher.

The best way to find a good and trustable contractor is to ask others for references. You can even take your realtor's help in finding a suitable and affordable contractor for your property.

Opt for Short-Term Rentals

A very normal practice in the real estate business is that investors buy some properties and then wait for their value to appreciate, so that they can sell it to earn great profits. However, everything is not so simple in the real estate market. Sometimes it takes several years for a property to appreciate in value, which only makes people lose money.

Because no one can manage several properties for a long period of time, they end up selling them for less than they bought them for. There are a few lucky ones who get to enjoy great profits by selling properties but it is usually not the case. So, if you are really into the idea of buying and selling properties, you should put them up for rent for a short-term.

Renting out properties is the safest and the perkiest option in the real estate business. Because your aim is to sell the properties once their values appreciate, you can make good money while the properties are still with you. Waiting for the market rates to increase is a gamble that every investor should avoiding taking. Instead of losing money every month, you will be earning lots of money in the form of rent. Once the market sees a high, you can plan on selling your properties to earn a lot more than you initially planned for.

Another thing that you need to keep in mind is that just like there are good days in the real estate market, there are bad ones too. There is a high chance that the value of your properties continues to depreciate, making you lose lots of money. In cases like these, investors are left with two options; either keep the properties and wait for the market to improve or simply sell their properties at very low rates.

Consider Vacation Rentals

When it comes to earning massive returns from your real estate investments, not many think about vacation rentals. The reason that investors and experts avoid suggesting this option is that it is again a huge risk. Furthermore, vacation homes can cost millions of dollars, which not everyone has.

However, if you look at it in term of ROI, you can give this option a shot. In order to earn huge returns from vacation homes, you need to pick a property in a highly desirable location. This means that you need to invest in communities that are near famous tourist spots. Of course the properties in such popular neighborhood will be extremely expensive. So, unless you have a lot to invest, don't opt for this option.

Let's talk about the good part now! When it comes to vacation homes, all you need to do is pick a good place and turn that property into a beautiful living space, and put it up for rent. The rent on vacation rentals is higher than normal homes because tourists are desperate to stay in a good place. In the peak vacation season, you will earn a lot. However, during less aggressive seasons, you might not get any guests at all.

Pre-Buy Condominiums and Sell for a Higher Price

The flashiest thing about investing in condominiums is that you get great returns. However, you need to buy the plots when the project is in the building process. Many contractors who build condominiums put the plots up for sale while the building is still in progress. The prices of plots in this time period are the lowest. So, you can get hold of really cheap plots in condominiums that can turn out to be great once the project is complete.

However, the thing that you need to keep in mind is that you pick the best condos to invest in. The contractors have a whole building plan and live models available for investors. So, before you invest in the condo, make sure you carefully examine everything and conduct proper research. You also need to make sure that the condo is in a good neighborhood and has necessary amenities within its enclosure or nearby. Factors like these will determine how much profit you will earn once the building is completed.

Sign a Lease for a Commercial Space

Leasing a commercial space is another great option for real estate investors that are looking to earn huge ROI. In order to make the most of this option, you need to pick a good commercial property in a business area.

Leasing is almost similar to renting out a property and earning rent. However, when it is a commercial property or an office space, it means that your tenants will be business owners. This gives you a great opportunity to earn a lot more than just the rent. Because it is a business, you can ask for a higher rent. This option also gives you a chance to increase the rent when the business is much more established.

Earning huge returns is not a piece of cake in the real estate business. However, if you know your ways, you can make the most of your initial investments. The different ways mentioned above will help you earn good return on your investment.

The thing about real estate is that it is a gamble. Only if you think smartly, you can earn massive. A great part of your business also depends on your connections. If you have solid connection in the market, you can sell your homes and market them in the most attractive way. You can also take help from a professional realtor, who will help find great buyers for you. Realtors are not just helpful in getting you buyers, but they can also get you reliable and affordable property managers and contractors.

Do not Expect a Magic to Happen

Many real estate investors end up disappointed when they expect too much. As part of this unpredictable business, you should understand there is no definitive formula to earn huge returns. You cannot just invest in a property and hope for it to be sold at a higher rate. You have to work hard to get what you are looking for.

If you will enter this business believing that it is full of perks, you will face disappointment. Be realistic with your expectations and if you really want to earn great returns, then spend time in the market, devise smart strategies, and put your efforts into the property, and only then you will get the results that you are looking for.

Chapter 14: Tips To Make Your Investment Property Look Perfect

One of the most important things that every real estate investor needs to keep in mind is that selling and renting properties is not the only way to earn great returns. Every real estate investor should know the importance of good looking and well-managed properties.

If you are already a part of the real estate business, you would know that many times you are about to sign a great deal with a buyer, but due to some issues in the property's aesthetic appeal, buyers simply pull-back their offer. This happens when you did not give enough time to improving the property's condition and looks.

Property management is an important part of every real estate investor's job. This business is not just about investing in several properties, but you have to really focus on making the property look appealing, which is the number one factor that helps get you good returns.

Let's take a look at the different ways you can enhance your property's overall appeal and look.

Part 1: The Exterior

The first thing that buyers observe in a property that they are about to purchase is its exterior look. Because when you are entering a property, you get to see its exterior first, which plays a crucial part in setting an impression. If a property looks alluring from the outside, the buyers instantly become interested in buying it.

However, if the property looks damaged or unappealing, the buyers might even refrain from checking it from the inside. Because of the external appearance, buyers might also make 90% of their decision. That's the reason it is important to ensure that the property that you are selling or renting out looks fascinating. So, how do you attract buyers through your property's exterior look? Let's find out!

Get it Cleaned!

The simplest way to instantly enhance the look of your property's exterior is to get it cleaned. Hire professional cleaners to clean the outdoor area of your property. If there is a driveway or a walking pathway outside the property, make sure it is clear of dirt, dust, and debris. If there is grass, trees, and bushes outside the property, make sure the dried leaves aren't sailing on the floor. You can also get the outdoor area washed with water to make it appear cleaner.

Trim the Bushes and Trees

Many homes are surrounded by trees and bushes. Although plants add greenery and freshness to any place, they can become quite unimpressive if not managed properly. So, if the outdoor area of your property consists of bushes and trees, make sure they are trimmed before the buyers visit the property. Properly shaped bushes are great for enhancing the curb appeal of any property, adding extra liveliness at the same time. Also make sure that the lawn is mowed.

Paint the Exterior Walls

Another thing that can make your property look hundred times more appealing is a new paint-job. Painting the exterior of a house is trickier than painting its interior. So, if you are having doubts, it's better to call a professional to do the job. A new paint-job makes the walls and home look fresh. This extra freshness will definitely help you get extra bucks from the buyers. Make sure that you get the entrance door painted too.

Fix the Windows and the Doors

Whether the house has wooden windows and doors or metal ones, you need to get them fixed before the buyers visit. Sometimes the windows and doors in a house are crooked or damaged, which makes the entire property seem old and shabby. Therefore, if you don't want the buyers to feel like they are purchasing an old and damaged home, make sure that you either install new windows and doors, or simply get them painted.

Replace the Main Door

The entrance door of a house plays a vital role in creating a lasting impression on the visitors. Therefore, when you are planning to sell the home, invest in a good quality wooden door for the home. There are a variety of impressive door styles available in the market. However, make sure that the door you pick matches the style of your home. Do not buy a modern door if the home is old style.

Consider Lighting

What if the buyers visit the property at night-time and are unable to look at the house clearly? This usually happens when sellers do not consider adding lights to the outdoor area. Lights play an important role in making a home look lively. Good lighting can really help create an impressive look for your property's exterior.

So, buy quality lights and add them in symmetry on the front porch or simply install a beautiful hanging lamp outside the door. If there is a garden or greenery outside the property, install dim lights to give the home a beautiful look. Make sure that you hide the lights in the bushes and plants instead of leaving them on show.

Add Some Greenery

Green plants and colorful flowers outside the house can instantly enhance its look and overall appeal. That's why, if you are looking to attract more buyers to your property, make sure you invest in good plants. However, do not take the idea wrong by adding too many plants outside the house, as it can make the house look scary. Furthermore, the plants that you add should be manageable. Pick the most attractive flowering plants and hire a gardener to do the job for you. If you have experience with gardening, make your own landscaped beds to make the exterior of your property look clean and appealing.

Alex Lee

Consider Your Neighbors' Homes

What if you make tweaks to your home and enhance its exterior appeal, but when buyers visit, they are not too happy with your neighbor's messy outdoors? This often happens when the homes besides your property are low on maintenance. Instead of fighting with your neighbors over the matter, try cleaning their outdoors as well. Because it is you who is trying to sell the property, you have to work on enhancing the look and feel of it. So, if there is a lot of debris outside the neighbor's house, clean it. If the neighbor's bushes are out of control, trim them. This will help you make the area surrounding your property look clean and tidy, which will attract more buyers.

Part 2: The Interior

The exterior of your property holds the most importance because it is the first thing that the buyers see. However, if the interior is crappy and damaged, do you think your exterior tweaks would work? Definitely not!

That's the reason when it is time to sell a property, it is important to work on both; the interior and exterior. When it comes to the interior of the property, you need to examine everything carefully. From different systems of the home to its appeal, everything should be considered. Let's take a look at the different areas you need to work on in the property's interior for making the property sell at a greater value.

Fix Damaged Systems

Every home buyer dreams of a home with a perfect drainage, water, cooling, and heating system. Because these systems are crucial for daily chores, fixing damages can also cost quite a lot. Sometimes small repairs also prove to be helpful in increasing the value of a property. Furthermore, if you fix small repairs in time, it helps keep you from a big repair project.

Even if a small pipe in the home is leaking, fix it. Little things like these help buyers feel relaxed that they are purchasing a perfect property, which will not require additional repairs.

Paint the Interior

A simple paint job can make any area look new and fresh. However, make sure you do not pick a dark color for the interior walls, as it will make the home look small and overwhelming. Pick earthy tones or pastel colors like tae pink and pistachio green. If you are unable to decide, go with the safest option and pick cream or off-white color for the walls. Cream and off-white colors are perfect for adding more life and space to any home. This color is also suitable for keeping the indoor environment cool. A new paint job will make the property look as good as new.

Conduct Major Cleaning

No one likes to visit a home which is untidy and poorly managed. So, if you don't want buyers to run away, clean the home. Cleaning an entire home might become hectic. So, it is better to hire a maintenance team to do the job. Make sure the floors and platforms are thoroughly scrubbed with detergent and water. You will also need to clean any glass or mirror in the house to ensure there are zero fingerprints. Make sure that the cleaning team also washes the carpets. A clean home looks, feels, and smells great too. So if you think that it is not needed, you are mistaken. A sparkling home will surely attract many buyers.

Increase Energy Efficiency inside the House

Nowadays, the thing that many buyers are looking for in a home is its energy efficiency. Energy efficient products not only have a minimum impact on the environment, but they are also great for saving money. So, if you want the value of your property to be increased, make sure you invest in good energy saving products like energy saving light bulbs and appliances.

Improve Insulation

The thing that disturbs homeowners the most is bad insulation. Bad insulation leads to poor cooling and heating inside the home, resulting in increased energy bills. So, if you want the buyers to feel relieved, then conduct proper inspection and improve insulation.

Although you can conduct the inspection on your own, it is best to call an energy efficiency auditor for the job. The main areas that you should check include the attic, windows, floors, and doors. If there are any cracks in the walls, windows, and floors, there is a high chance that the heating and cooling systems won't work that well.

Cracked windows and doors should be immediately replaced or fixed. If the walls and ceiling has seepage, call a home improvement team to fix it for you. Fixes and improvements like these add instant value to any home, making it sell at a higher rate.

Upgrading the House

Apart from the usual home improvement chores, you can invest in upgrades to make your home sell at top dollar. However, if you have a tight budget, it is better to stay away from this option because it can cost a lot of money. In case you are interested, we have a list of areas that can add value to the home.

Kitchen Upgrade

Kitchens have become more like living rooms in today's homes. Families are spending more time in their kitchens, making it the most popular spot in the home. So, a simple makeover of the kitchen can sell your home at a great value.

The main idea behind a kitchen upgrade should be to make it more relaxing. Add stools under the kitchen counters, so that everyone can chat while one of the members cooks food. Apart from stools, you also need to focus on adding a granite or marble countertop. This material is extremely popular for adding an extra oomph to the kitchen. Furthermore, these materials are also easy to clean.

When it comes to appliances, make sure you buy stainless steel ones. Stainless steel gives the kitchen a highly modern and sleek look. Add a hanging lamp above the countertop to make the kitchen look more attractive. A kitchen upgrade like this will help you attract many buyers offering a good price for the home.

Bathroom Upgrade

Toilet spaces catch every buyer's attention. That's the reason upgrading a toilet space is something that you should consider investing in. A crooked and dirty bathroom will send alarming signals to the buyers who visit the property. By adding a simple window in the bathroom, you can make more way for natural light to enter, making the toilet look more spacious and airy.

You should also check the tub in the toilet to see if it is in perfect shape. If the tub is scratched or rugged, make sure you get it reglazed. Reglazing helps make the tub look new, without costing a lot of money. Updates like these will make your home look more valuable, helping you earn greater profit.

Appliance Upgrade

Old and worn appliances can make any home look dull. Moreover, clean and shining appliances make buyers feel relaxed that they are investing in a home that doesn't require a lot of fixes and repairs. If you invest in upgrading the appliances, you can get a great return on it.

Furthermore, if all the appliances in the home don't match, it might make the home look chaotic. Opt for similar style appliances like the stainless steel ones for creating a harmonized look inside the home. A little investment like this will turn the interior around, making it appear alluring and extremely modern. Appliance replacement also means that the buyers will not need to invest in new ones any time soon.

If a complete appliance replacement doesn't fit your budget, then call the service team to get them cleaned and polished. If there are some odd-looking appliances, replace those only.

Making small or major changes to a property is helpful in making you earn increased profit out of your investment property, especially if you are selling or renting it. The more efforts you put in the property, the more you are going to get in return.

Chapter 15: Mistakes Every Real Estate Investor Should Avoid

Every real estate investor is looking to earn that extra cash, but what they fail to realize is that one wrong step can result in a major drop. Many investors have made several mistakes in the past, which have helped us stay more alert and careful while taking decisions regarding our properties. Selling or renting out a home might seem easy at first, but if you do not pay attention to the details, it might turn into your worst nightmare.

In order to avoid losing money, you should be careful while taking decisions related to your properties. Let's take a look at some of the most common investor mistakes that you need to avoid.

Mistakes Investors Make When Selling a Property

Selling a home isn't an easy job. You need to have proper market knowledge to come up with great strategies. However, if you don't give time to devising solid strategies, you might end up making these common mistakes that investors make. Let's take a look at the most common mistakes that investors make when selling their properties.

Selling the Property without any Help

It is alright to feel confident about your decisions, but being overconfident can make you lose money. The biggest and the most common mistake that investors maker is selling their properties without taking help from the experts. For Sale By Owner are those properties that are directly sold by the owners.

FSBO properties might help you earn lots of profit, but it can also get tricky. When you don't have enough market knowledge and insight, you are unable to make the right decision. There are several factors that you need to consider before you put your property up for sale. These factors include price, value, home improvements, and legalities. If you fail to take any one of these factors into account, you will make bad strategies.

So, hiring a professional realtor is the best option for investors looking to maximize their profits.

Selling the Property in Winter

If you have a little know-how of the real estate market, you'd know that winter season is not good for selling homes. However, many investors end up making this huge mistake. Winter seasons means snow covered roads and houses. Moreover, due to the chilled weather, people avoid heading outdoors. Therefore, if you put up your home for sale in the winter season, you will face disappointment.

Selling a property in winter means fewer buyers. This will delay your home selling process and the buyers that make an offer will be looking to get the home at a lower price. So, if earning great returns is your goal, then avoid selling your property during the winter season.

Pricing the Home too High

Because every investor is looking to earn more profit, they fail to appropriately price their property. This is a huge problem in the real estate market, as many investors price their homes at a high price. Regardless of the neighborhood, any home listed above market rate is not easily sold. This common concept is often overlooked by investors that choose to go solo.

Asking a high price for a home will not make you earn profit, but it will keep your property from selling. Furthermore, the buyers that visit will ask for a justification for the high price, which you will be unable to give. So, make sure you conduct proper research on the neighborhood, and then decide a price for the home based on the rates of other properties.

Getting Angry on Buyers

Many sellers get offended when buyers make a lowball offer. Taking offense and getting angry at the buyers will only spread a bad word about you in the market. As investors, you need to understand that buyers will be looking to buy the property in the lowest possible rate. So, if you get a really low offer, do not get aggressive, and take it as a business deal. Be calm and try to negotiate the rates.

This is a chance to exhibit your great negotiation powers and if the buyers do not show flexibility, you have the right to say no. Losing your temper will only make you look bad, spreading negative feedback in the market. When other buyers will hear about your attitude, they will not prefer offering a deal to you.

Not Investing in Marketing

Just like any other product or service, properties also require marketing. Many investors make the mistake of not investing in marketing, which results in few buyers approaching your property.

If you don't market your property, how would anyone come to know that there is a property up for sale? This means that you need to work on marketing. Having connections with realtors also helps market your property to prospect buyers. Furthermore, if you are looking to earn great returns from your property, you need to make it visible to a maximum number of people. Find out effective marketing tips for your real estate property in the next chapter.

Over-Investing on Upgrades

Every realtor or expert that you meet will tell you about the importance of upgrading the property before putting it up on the market. It is true that upgrades make homes sell at a higher rate, but over-upgrading the property can have an opposite effect.

Upgrades are fine if you spend in a limit, but if you put in a lot of money in making the house look appealing, you might exceed the property's current market value, which will keep it from selling.

As real estate investors, you should be aware of how different neighborhoods and markets work. If you upgrade a property located in an average neighborhood, you will not get high offers on it. Buyers always buy homes after comparing them with other properties in the neighborhood. Therefore, spending extra money on improvements and renovation might prove useless. Spend wisely and avoid making unnecessary changes to the property.

Not Making Use of Resources

Many investors believe that putting up a notice outside the house that the property is up for sale does the job. However, buyers are no longer walking through neighborhoods to look for properties, but they make use of the Internet to check photos of properties on sale. This means that if you are not making use of online resources to list your property, you are missing out on a greater chunk of potential buyers.

Mistakes Investors Make When Putting a Property Up for Rent

Renting out a property might seem the most profitable decisions, but if made without proper planning, it can cause a lot of loss. Because renting out a property earn you a greater cash flow, you need to keep in mind these common mistakes that investors make.

Not Screening the Tenants

Renting out a property is complicated, and requires a lot of diligence. However, what many investors fail to realize is that all tenants don't have the right intention. If you lack market knowledge and experience, the tenants you meet might take it in their advantage.

While you are busy managing and finalizing the legal paperwork, the tenants might disappear into thin air. That's the reason it is important to conduct a background check on prospect tenants interested in renting your property. You should get in touch with realtors to look for the tenants' past records and find if they are trustworthy or not. Without a proper background check, you might end up losing money or getting fooled by your tenants.

Failing to Keep up with the Tenants

As a landlord, you should be in control of your properties and the tenants. Leaving your tenants unattended might end up in bad surprises. So, make it a habit of visiting your tenants once every month. Surprise visits like these will allow you to be aware of your property's condition. If tenants have made a mess of your property, you can talk to them about it. It is best to hire a property manager to look after your properties and tenants.

Other Common Real Estate Investor Mistakes

Apart from the mistakes made when selling or renting out a property, investors make many other mistakes that lead to loss. Let's find out below!

Not Hiring a Property Manager

Whether you are selling your property or renting it out, if you have several properties to look after, do not forget to hire a property manager. Many investors want to save the maximum amount of money, which often leads to greater losses. The biggest money-saving mistake is to manage all the properties without taking help from a professional.

When you own several properties, it is hard to look after each one of it on your own. Managing properties becomes even harder when you rent them out. There are renters you have to deal with and their never-ending problems. Property managers on the other hand are professionals at managing properties and ensuring that they are in perfect shape. With these professionals looking after your properties, you will minimize maintenance and repair costs, and get a hassle-free communication system in place for the tenants.

Not Keeping the Property Well-Maintained

What happens to a poorly maintained property? It doesn't sell at a good price. So, if you are one of those investors who think that selling the property in the same condition as you bought it in is going to make you earn good bucks, you are sadly mistaken.

Every property is prone to physical damage. When you don't maintain your property, its appearance deteriorates. The buyers will offer only little price for such a property because they have to invest in repairs and improvements on their own. A well maintained property on the other hand is free of any damage, which means that the buyers will be willing to offer a good deal.

Assuming you will Get Rich Immediately

Did you enter into the real estate business assuming that you will be earning easy cash? Real estate investors that are new to the business often mistake it as a way to earn good money in no time. What they don't know is that in order to earn big, you need to learn about the market and take several chances until you get there. You cannot just buy one property and think that selling it at a higher price will mark you as a successful real estate investor. An investor with this thought will get disappointed pretty soon in their business career.

If you want to assume something, assume that it will be hard to earn big bucks in this business. Expect little and you will be surprised when you get more than you anticipated. The disappointment that comes with assuming will make it hard for you to stick in the market.

Not Having an Investment Plan

Without a plan you will end up making bad business decisions in the real estate business. Because it is all about your money, you need to make strategies. You should clearly know what you want and what to say no to. However, being a perfectionist in this business will always keep you unsatisfied.

Set criteria for investing in properties. This criterion will help you pick the best properties and earn good returns. If you don't have criteria, you will be confused between yes or no. You cannot just purchase any property. You should develop well defined financial criteria. This will keep you from making bad investment decisions. Furthermore, do not make the mistake of putting all your money into investment because if you fail, you will lose it all.

Purchasing a Property with Negative Cash Flow

It might sound surprising, but there are many investors who make the mistake of investing in properties with negative cash flow. This usually happens when there is a cheap property on the market and you want to make the most of it. Investors buy such properties in hopes that one day its value will appreciate, earning them lots of profit.

Buying a property with negative cash flow is a huge gamble that you might want to avoid taking. The investors that do so often end up waiting for several years. In the end they are only left with one option; to leave the property and sell it at a very low rate. These properties take a whole lifetime to appreciate in value, which means that the owners have to spend a lot of money on them.

As real estate investors, you should take lesson from the mistakes done by other investors. The mistakes mentioned in this chapter are common in this business. By learning from these mistakes, you will be able to make better decisions that will automatically lead to greater returns.

Chapter 16: Earning Great Returns Through Effective Marketing

If brands did not market their products and services, would you know what is new in the stores? Everyone who runs a business has to invest in marketing. Without marketing, every business would suffer losses. That's right.

So, what makes you think that marketing isn't essential in the real estate business? Well, if you try to sell a property without telling everyone about it, how can you expect prospect buyers to visit? However, there are many investors who still don't buy this idea and believe that marketing is just a waste of money.

When you market a property, you attract lots of buyers. Marketing is extra important for those investors who do not have a realtor by their side. Because realtors themselves act as marketing agents due to their connections, many investors don't feel the need to market separately when they have already hired a realtor.

So, whether you are selling your property or putting it up for rent, it is important to consider investing in marketing. Let's take a look at the different ways an investor can market their properties for great returns.

Make use of the Internet

In this digitally advanced era, it is hard to not consider Internet as one of the most powerful marketing tools. Millions of brands and businesses are making use of this platform to reach out to their customers. Furthermore, a recent study conducted by the National Association of Realtors revealed that almost 92% of the buyers look for properties on the Internet.

This is a huge indication that people choose Internet as their primary source for house-hunting. So, if you want to sell or rent out your property, better make use of the Internet. However, make sure you pick the most appropriate and highest traffic generating real estate house listing sites. Zillow is one of the most attractive platforms to market your property to attract heaps of buyers and renters to your properties.

Google Adwords

Another great way to market your properties through internet is to make use of Google Adwords. All you need to do is design an ad and pay Google to make it visible on its search engine. However, one thing that discriminates a good ad from a bad one is the keyword choice. Keywords are phrases that you add to your ad, which makes it easily searchable. Let's say you pick the keywords 'house for sale in California' and 'house for rent in California', and when a user types in this phrase, they will be able to see your ad. This is a great way to reach out to your potential target audience and make your properties sell.

Create an Intriguing Video

Interesting videos often go viral on the internet within a few hours. Thanks to social sharing plugins that users can use to easily share videos from one platform to another, spreading them all over the Internet like wildfire.

So, if you feel that a little text is not enough to describe the awesomeness of your property, make a video. Make sure that the video is interesting. You can exhibit the great features of your home and give the buyers a reason to purchase your property. You can also ask your friends and family to share the video on their social networks, which will increase its viewability, allowing you to get good results.

Use Craigslist

People visit Craigslist for buying and selling things. This platform has a huge client base, which means that when you put up your property on it, it will be viewed by a lot of people. This marketing tool will help bring more people to your property, allowing you to negotiate a good deal.

Design your Own Website

You are a real estate investor, which means that you are buying and selling properties. So, just like any other business, you also need to consider launching your very own website. When you have your own website, you get to talk about your properties and market them more effectively. However, in order to get more people to visit your website, you need to have a proper online marketing strategy in place. Dig deep into Search Engine Optimization and look for tools that can help make your website stand-out. Your main purpose should be to drive relevant traffic to your website, and you will be able to do so if your website is on a good rank on the Google search engine.

You can bring your website on a good rank by making use of SEO tools and techniques like keywords, backlinks, content marketing, and much more. Once you have successfully set-up your online presence, your target audience will know where to head if they have to buy or rent properties.

Write Attractive Listing Description

Listing descriptions play an important role in bringing in potential buyers. Many sellers and investors believe that adding beautiful pictures of the property is enough to make it sell, but what they fail to realize is that the description of the property itself can be the selling point.

But what do you really write in the description? Well, if you are thinking that mentioning the number of rooms and bathrooms is enough to attract buyers, then you are sadly mistaken. Of course the buyers would like to know the number of rooms and bathroom in the property, but they would love to find out the minor details.

So, if you don't have good creative writing skills, hire a writer to do the job for you. The description should emphasize on things like flooring material, appliance style, yard size, and the features in the kitchen. If you have made use of specific brands, mention the name as it will help make your property seem more valuable and credible.

Example Listing Description

Wake up to the Scenic Views of the Lake

Step into a spacious home located in front of a beautiful lake, surrounded by lush green land. If that's not enough for you, then you can enjoy in your personal enclosed garden that adds to the beauty of the exterior space. Recently remodeled, this home has three huge sized bedrooms with attached luxurious bathrooms. Classy stainless steel appliances and granite countertops make the kitchen a small hang-out place while you are cooking for the family or guests.

You will no longer be driving several miles to buy grocery or dine-out, because the commercial areas are at walking distance. The detached two car garage is perfect for the ones who want a little more space. The newly added hardwood floors make the home look totally fabulous.

There is no chance that anyone who takes a tour of this two- story home does not fall in love with it.

Don't believe it? Come by and find out for yourself!

Hurry up before you miss our amazing lease-purchase option!

Get in Touch with a Realtor

Real estate agents are professionals that have several years of experience in the real estate market. They also have lots of contacts and connections, which prove to be helpful for investors looking to sell or rent out their properties. So, if you are looking to attract potential buyers and renters to your property, you can get in touch with a realtor. Although it's an old school method of marketing, it is still very effective. These realtors also help spread a good word about you in the market, which helps attract many buyers.

Post a Classified Ad in the Newspaper

If you think that no one reads newspaper anymore, then you are mistaken. There is a huge chunk of the population that still reads onto the ads posted in newspapers. By posting an ad in the newspaper, you will be able to attract lots of buyers. The people that purchase homes belong to the segment that religiously reads newspapers. So, don't underestimate this powerful marketing tool.

Place a Sign outside the Property

Placing a sign outside the property might be an old marketing tool, but it is definitely an effective one. When people are looking to purchase or rent a property, they visit different neighborhoods looking for homes. By adding a simple 'for sale' or 'for rent' sign outside the property, you can attract more people.

Design Flyers and distribute them

Another great tool for marketing your properties and attracting more buyers and tenants is to get catchy flyers designed by a professional designer. Many big brands design flyers and then give them out to people on the streets to spread a message or advertise a product/service. The good part about using flyers as an advertising and marketing tool is that you get to pick the audience. So, if you believe that your target audience lives in a particular community, distribute the flyers there. Don't forget to add photos of the property, its features, and your contact information in the flyer. A little catchy description will be perfect for making your property standout.

The real estate market is continually becoming more challenging and competitive. In order to maintain your position in the market, every investor needs to invest money on advertising and marketing. Marketing your property will help you reach a greater target audience, allowing you to seal the perfect deal.

Chapter 17: Managing Real Estate Risks

Contrary to what others say, real estate is really a business packed with risks. However, if you are aware of the risks that are involved with it, you will be able to make your investment as safe as possible. Of course if you enter this business assuming that you will earn big money and turn minimum investments into huge returns, then you are definitely mistaken.

As an investor, you will be looking to earn maximum profits, but you need to measure all the risks before you make any big financial decision. Let's take a look at the common risks in the real estate business that will help you learn to stay cautious.

Do Not Pay More than You Can Afford

Real estate investments seem really perky to the ones who don't have experience in this market. Such people often end up investing in a property they find interesting, not considering their affordability. Because there are so many options available for borrowing money, many investors choose to take a loan to purchase a property that they otherwise wouldn't have been able to afford.

What happens when you buy a property from borrowed money is that instead of earning from it, you end up paying a lot of money in mortgage repayments. So, even when you rent your property out, you still give a greater chunk of that income to the lenders. This means that you will have a negative cash flow and you will not be earning the money that you thought you'd be.

Invest in Properties with Positive Cash Flow

When investing in a property, make sure you give enough time to planning and considering the income that you are going to get in return. If you buy a property that pays for itself in the form of income you generate from it, then it's profitable. But if the property does not produce enough income to cover your costs and the investment amount, you need to look for alternate options or else you'll end up with a huge loss.

Buying an Overpriced Property

Investing in an overpriced property might seem like a good decision, but if you sit down and think about it, you are actually taking a huge risk. The people who are looking to purchase or rent a property want to sign the most profitable deal, which means that they will be looking for the lowest figure. Selling or renting out an overpriced property means that you will be looking to earn profit by pricing it high (higher than you purchased it for).

Overpriced properties are harder to sell because no one is ready to invest a huge amount of money. Even when you rent it out, you will be expecting to rent it on a high rate and no one will be willing to pay it. So, all you will be left with will be managing and maintaining the property, resulting in poor cash flow. In fact, this will result in a huge financial loss.

Start with Lower Rent

When you are renting your property for the first time, start by asking for a lower rent. Demanding a lower rent for your property will also allow you to attract many tenants. A lower rent strategy will also help you increase the rent once the tenants have settled. If you will ask for a higher rent from the start, you will face disappointments when no one will be willing to rent the house.

Don't Borrow a Loan you cannot Repay

Sometimes investors aren't looking to invest in a property but then they find a fabulous deal that they cannot ignore. This is a common scenario in the real estate market, but when you make hasty decisions like these, you do not realize that they can put a long-lasting dent on your finances.

What many investors do is borrow a loan from lenders for a property that they cannot seem to let go. Furthermore, they don't even design a loan repayment strategy that causes trouble in the long run. When these investors fail to make regular loan repayments, the lenders file for foreclosure. This way, you not only lose the property but also lots of money.

So, even if the property is out-of-the-world, do not borrow a loan that you cannot repay. If you have a flowing income from your other investments, only then think about taking a loan.

Avoid Making Frequent Switches

Every investor has one thing in mind; to earn great returns. What they fail to understand is that flipping and switching properties too often can lead to minimum benefits. First of all, if you sell a property within three years, it comes under short-term capital gains, which means that you do not get to enjoy tax exemptions.

Flipping properties too often comes under business income, which is taxable. So, if you really want to keep the maximum profit to yourself, try not to switch properties too often. Keep the property for more than three years, work on it or just put it up for rent to earn a flowing income out of it.

Don't Put All of your Money at Risk

Property prices have no limits. You can invest as much money as you like, but don't make this mistake. Using all your savings to invest in a property is a stupid decision. The real estate market has its fair share of risks. If your investments did not work the way you planned, you will end up losing your money. Because you used your savings in the business, you will be left with nothing. So, do not make rash decisions when you are in the real estate business. Pre-plan everything and focus on minimizing the risks.

If you are looking for a good experience in the real estate business, then you need to measure all the risks before making any decision. Real estate investments involve a lot of money, which is why it is better to conduct proper research before risking it all.

Chapter 18: Effective Tips To Lower Landlording Risks

Apart from flipping properties, another common practice amongst investors is putting their properties up for rent. Renting out a property is a good option, especially for the investors that want to earn a flowing income.

However, when it comes to becoming a landlord, not many investors are aware of the pain it can be. Landlords are often irritated by their tenants that call them late in the night just to tell them that a pipe is leaking. Of course no one likes to be disturbed, and that's the reason every landlord needs to learn the ways to deal with risks involved with landlording. Let's take a look at some effective tips that will help you lower the risks and enjoy a trouble-free landlording experience.

Get your Property Insured

Giving your property to someone else to live in is a huge risk. Therefore, every landlord should consider getting their properties insured before the tenants walk in. Sometimes tenants make a lot of mess out of a property, damaging the house to a level that it takes up a lot of landlord's money. So, before you put the property up for rent, make sure you get in touch with your mortgage broker or real estate agent to discuss insurance options. Once your property is insured, you can relax as most of the damages will be covered by the insurance provider.

Make Sure that the Property is Safe for Living

What if your tenants get hurt or in trouble for living in your property? Well, if this happens, you can be hit with a lawsuit, which can easily damage your real estate investment portfolio. If you don't want this to happen to you, get in touch with an experienced realtor who can help you find out whether the property is safe to live in or not. Furthermore, you should conduct proper research on the environment and climate of the particular area your property lies in. This research will help ensure that the tenants will be living worry-free in your property, keeping you safe from hefty fines. You also need to ensure that your property meets all the health and safety codes for the area it is situated in.

Devise an Action Plan for Disaster Control

What if there is a flood in the neighborhood where you have rented out a property? Have you prepared your property from natural calamities like floods and thunderstorm? Do you have an action plan for fire incidents?

Well, if you did not think about these details before, then you need to start now. Any type of disaster will not only damage your property but it will also put your tenants in danger. Install fire safety equipment inside the house to ensure that the tenants will be safe. Additions like these also help increase the value of a property. So, don't hesitate and get your property inspected for disaster and emergency preparedness.

Apart from emergency occurrences like these, you also need to prepare your tenant contract and make a copy of it in case it gets damaged or lost. Other things that require special care include mortgage and property manager contract.

Ensure that the Neighborhood is Safe

What if someone breaks into the property and robs off your tenants? Wouldn't you be held responsible for overlooking your tenants' safety?

When you purchase a property and plan to rent it out, you need to ensure that the surrounding area is safe. It is better to be cautious when you purchase a property by conducting proper research about the neighborhood. Talk to other neighbors and ask them about the area. The houses that you rent out should be in a crime-free zone, because this will help protect your tenants from theft and loss.

It is also a good idea to invest in a security system for your property, which will keep it safe from burglars and thieves. Another factor that you need to consider when screening tenants is to ensure that they are not criminals. Also make sure that the property manager you hire to look after your properties is decent. When you perform an extensive background check of everything from tenants to the neighborhood, you are able to minimize security risks and concerns.

Manage Tenant Complaints in a Timely Manner

The biggest problem that landlords face is getting bombarded by calls from tenants. Tenants often contact landlords when they want to get an issue fixed. If you are irritated by these frequent calls, you can hire a property manager. Property managers are trained to deal with tenants. They also handle tenant complaints including maintenance and repair issues.

When you handle tenant complaints in a timely manner, you are automatically keeping them satisfied, which results in improved tenant-landlord relation, and increased tenant retention ratio.

When you take the role of a landlord, it is important to keep in mind that you have to have good managerial skills. Because you have to look after your tenants, properties, and other employees, you have a greater responsibility at hand. Therefore, if you want this experience to be smooth and trouble-free, make sure you keep on mind the points mentioned above.

Wrap Up!

Investing in real estate is a huge earning opportunity. Therefore, it is common for anyone to be interested in investing in it. Although this business helps you earn huge returns, it can also be extremely risky if you do not have proper strategies in place.

When you are becoming a part of this highly attractive business, you need to realize that it requires a lot of money. There are many options that one can consider if they don't have enough cash to invest in their desired property. However, when you borrow a loan, you have to ensure that you can pay it back.

Because everyone who invests in properties wants to earn huge returns, you need to come up with great strategies to turn your dreams into reality. Real estate investments are hard on the pocket, but once you get the hang of this market, you can really turn the numbers around and make a lot of money. It is also important to have a sound exit-strategy for every investment that you make.

If you are new to this business, you might want to take help from a professional investor that knows how this market works. If you get in touch with a good real estate investor, you will be able to get your hands on the most attractive and profitable properties in the market. Furthermore, taking help from experienced realtors should never be considered a disgrace by the investors. Realtors are people who have been working in the market for years. They have dealt with different types of buyers and sellers, and they know which strategies work the best.

Once you've spent enough time with qualified investors and worked on different strategies, you get one step closer to achieving your long-lost dream. This will be the time when you will be multiplying your investment amount and earning huge ROI. Moreover, make sure that you try different tactics and then pick the one that earned you success. Make use of this strategy and refine your choices to become a great real estate investor.

Remember, even when you have established your business, don't be negligent or over-confident with your decisions. No matter how many success stories you created, you still have a lot of room to learn in the real estate business.

Good luck and make sure you are investing in properties with the highest return on investment.

Printed in the United States
By Bookmasters